YOUR
IN 1

TAURUS

April 21 to May 21

ROGER ELLIOT

Futura

A Futura Book

Copyright © Roger Elliot 1988

First published in Great Britain in 1988
by Futura Publications, a Division of
Macdonald & Co (Publishers) Ltd
London & Sydney

ISBN 0 7088 3774 3

Photoset in North Wales by
Derek Doyle & Associates, Mold, Clwyd.
Reproduced, printed and bound in Great Britain by
Hazell Watson & Viney Limited
Member of BPCC plc
Aylesbury Bucks

Futura Publications
A Division of
Macdonald & Co (Publishers) Ltd
Greater London House
Hampstead Road
London NW1 7QX

A member of Maxwell Pergamon Publishing Corporation plc

Contents

ROGER ELLIOT is one of the top astrologers in the world today. As a writer, TV performer, teacher and consultant to many individuals, he spans the full range of astrology from scientific research to newspaper columns.

Roger, born on June 25 under the sign of Cancer, lives in a Somerset manor house with his blonde Leo wife Suzie, and two teenage children, Stephanie (Aries) and Mark (Aquarius) – not forgetting the two Sagittarian Jack Russell terriers.

My World
of Astrology

Welcome once more to my series of Zodiac books – this time for 1989 – and greetings to all my readers throughout the world.

It's a privilege to be able to guide you through the trials and pitfalls – yes, and the joys and successes – lying ahead of you in the next twelve months. Basically the last year of the decade will be pretty good for you and the rest of the Zodiac signs, and I think a great many people will make excellent progress before we reach the 1990s.

Remember that the daily forecasts are written in two sections. The first half, *written in italic,* refers to the whole world and everyone in it. They give you an idea how other people are likely to behave on the day in question – indeed, they may give a clue to the national and international events taking place. I well remember how the Chernobyl explosion several years ago took place when the Sun was opposite Pluto, meaning 'the end of one chapter and the beginning of a new one'.

The second half of each daily forecast refers, as usual, to yourself – as a birth-child of Taurus – and the moods, events and circumstances that may occur in your individual life. Sometimes they match the generalized forecast, but sometimes they differ, simply because the planets that day are making a special pattern as far as your Zodiac sign is concerned.

Once again I've included Wise Words at the end of each monthly group of predictions. Most of them are wry or funny, so don't take them too seriously, but each of them does refer, however obliquely, to the mood of the month.

As before, the section Mixing with Others enables you to see how you relate to each of the twelve Zodiac signs. Perhaps it will help you to understand personal links more clearly, whether it's a friendship, a sexual partnership, a relative or business contact.

Obviously I must remind you that this series of books is

written for the world, not just your neck of the woods. I have to reach the mind and touch the heart of everyone from New York to New Zealand, and all of you are leading different lives, with your own problems, challenges and hopes, and to those who don't believe in astrology that's an end to it.

But *we* know differently – myself because I've studied astrology for half my life now, and you, whoever you are, because you chose to pick up this book. Something drew you. Something prompted you. It wasn't a total accident.

Some of you have been my friends and readers for many years. Others will be beginning this friendship for the first time now, because believe me – followers of astrology are a world-wide fellowship that is linked by the certainty that there is a guiding hand in our lives, nudging us this way and that.

Exactly what these influences may be, and how they work, is an endlessly complex study, which is why you must take my words in the spirit in which they're offered – as a guide, but no more, to the way your life may develop during 1989.

You must take your individual circumstances into account, and realize that the possibility of illness, for example, won't happen to *every* Taurus person.

Please don't think that I believe that we are fated to act out our lives according to the dictates of the stars. We do have free will. We may not always be able to control the circumstances around us, but we can control our *response* to them.

We all know saintly people who may be poor, lonely or ill but still seem to radiate happiness and, more important, a kind of inner vitality that cheers up the rest of us. Equally we know Mr and Mrs Grouch who, surrounded by the best of everything, still manage to complain!

I hope astrology can help you to place your life in some kind of broader framework. I hope it allows you to see a wider perspective to existence. It is difficult – and unfashionable – for many people to believe that life has a pattern and a purpose. But those of us who know differently are quite sure that, to echo the words of Hamlet, 'there are more things in heaven and earth than are dreamt of'.

To understand this pattern, I use computers to analyse the

celestial movements and store an ever-increasing amount of information from you – the readers of this book. It does help greatly if you can write telling me which forecasts are true, using the address on page 95. In this way I am constantly updating my information, so that future books can be even more detailed and, hopefully, correct.

Obviously, in a book of this size, referring to so many kinds of people – mothers, businessmen, school-kids, pensioners and so forth – there will be remarks that may not refer directly to you. Well, be patient – and, if necessary, use your imagination to change the precise meaning into one that could refer to your individual circumstances.

And do remember that I'm always willing to help with personal problems. If you want to learn more about astrology, and get your own horoscope in some way, turn to page 94 for further details. Wherever you live, whatever your difficulties, your letter will reach me.

It's easy for those of us who are happy to become smug and complacent about life. But think of the Earth circling the Sun, as a child circles its father. Think of the Moon circling us, as a mother enfolds her child in love and cherishing.

We are surrounded by a family of planets, each one capable of making contact with our own inmost being.

We are not alone. We live in an invisible world of forces that subtly encourage us in one direction, discourage us in another – all in accordance with our true destiny.

May you find peace and fulfilment in the year ahead. And may this Taurus book guide your path.

God bless you, my friend.

ROGER ELLIOT

Technical Note

Some people think that astrology is all psychic intuition, but it's a good deal more scientific than that.

First of all, using my computers, I prepare an *ephemeris* for 1989 listing the positions of the Sun and planets, together with all their midpoints, for each day of the year. They are grouped along a great circle in the sky called the *ecliptic* or Zodiac, which is divided into the twelve signs.

Then I prepare a daily *aspectarian* telling which planets are in line with each other, or in opposition, or square to each other, or whatever it may be. Let's take New Year's Day as an example. On January 1 Mercury is trine Jupiter, while the Sun is conjunction Neptune. These are just two of thirteen aspects in force that day.

Now each planet represents a different quality in life. So Mercury stands for communication, while Jupiter stands for happiness. So it's a broadly pleasant day, but the Sun-Neptune contact means there will be some deception or muddle, especially within the family circle.

That's why my general prediction for this festive day on page 36 is *Slightly argumentative, but happy on the whole. Family squabbles, perhaps.* In fact, the Sun-Neptune aspect could produce a world event involving deception.

The individual forecast that follows is based on a careful analysis of what these planets mean for Taurus. Sometimes I am very scientific, noting the rulerships of the planets as far as you are concerned, and sometimes I simply get a mental picture of the various conflicting forces and imagine how a person like yourself would respond.

So it's a mixture of science and imagination – I hope! At all events, I trust it will be helpful to you.

Mixing
with Others

You may think that just because you're a Taurus person you have got nothing in common with Virgo or Capricorn.

But in fact these three signs have a lot in common, because all the Zodiac signs are linked by an enthralling system of Elements and Modes. By discovering which Mode and Element you belong to, you can find out what you have in common with other signs – and what you don't!

The Modes

Aries, Cancer, Libra and Capricorn belong to the Cardinal Mode. All the Cardinal signs are concerned with activity. In their differing ways they like to get things moving; to take practical steps; to start a new enterprise. So they resemble the cardinal points of the compass – north, south, east and west – in the sense that they point in a new direction.

Taurus, Leo, Scorpio and Aquarius belong to the Fixed Mode. Fixed signs are exactly what they say they are: immovable and fixed, gaining strength from maintaining a situation rather than changing it. They have the virtue of persistence and the drawback of stubbornness.

If the Cardinal signs can be symbolized by a pointing finger, Fixed signs are represented by a clenched fist.

Gemini, Virgo, Sagittarius and Pisces belong to the Mutable Mode. Mutable signs express changeability. They are also called dualistic signs because their energy seems to fluctuate.

If Cardinal signs drive straight down the road, Mutable ones veer from side to side. This provides great flexibility of outlook, but also great unreliability and lack of constancy.

The Elements

Capricorn, Taurus and Virgo belong to the **Earth Element.**

9

Earth signs are solid, reliable and stable. The world tends to approve of earthy people, although they can be rather crude and indelicate at times. We like their common sense.

The drawback of these signs is their lack of enterprise and vision. They can become encased in materialism, and gradually action can become clogged by inertia.

Aries, Leo and Sagittarius belong to the **Fire Element**. All the Fire signs have a magical quality, enabling them to fire other people into activity. At their most creative, these signs have constant access to real enthusiasm. They are powered by an unending fuel store helping them to achieve a great deal. At their most destructive, however, the Fire signs use other people as fuel. They burn the energy out of them, leaving behind a trail of wrecked hearts.

Libra, Aquarius and Gemini belong to the **Air Element**. Air is an insubstantial Element. It breezes this way and that, carrying seeds from one part of the land to another. Traditionally it's linked with the transmission of ideas.

Air signs are communicative and sociable – bringing men and women together; spreading ideas and trying to change their surroundings. You can see the possible faults of these signs in the popular sayings 'too airy-fairy' or 'talking a lot of hot air'.

Cancer, Scorpio and Pisces belong to the **Water Element**. Water is the most mysterious of the four Elements. We are said to be born in the waters of the womb, or have evolved from earlier aquatic creatures, and spiritually we return to the great waters of eternity.

Water signs have a fine capacity to flow into the hearts and minds of other people. Like electricity through water, they are conducive to the ideas and feelings coming their way, and they respond very sensitively to their environment.

At worst, of course, they are wet, drippy and sloppy!

Aries
March 21 to April 20

Friendships Aries people like friends but hate to be dependent on them. They are self-reliant folk who, in the last resort, are quite happy on their own. They take friends at face value, and don't like people who are too moody or changeable or hanging back from making decisions. They enjoy the company of people who are enthusiastic, good-humoured and brave – just like themselves, in fact!

Sex Aries people are sexy, but that doesn't make them all Don Juans or nymphomaniacs. They have a strong, muscular sex nature that likes to impose itself on others. If anything, their sexuality is stronger than their need for love. Certainly they are self-centred people, and can ignore their partners' feelings.

Marriage Aries folk are not settlers by nature, but more like nomads or hunters. There's more fun for them in making new conquests than sticking with the same old mate. On the other hand, they hate failure – and what they have, they hold. So they can make loyal, stable marriage partners. If the marriage does get stale, Aries is the one to put a stop to the agony.

Aries (March 21 to April 20) and You

Surprisingly harmonious. You look for peace and security but are livened up by fiery Aries. Can be highly sexy!

With an **Aries friend** you don't share many hobbies, and your opinions are miles apart. But you have a basic fondness for each other. 1989 rating: take life easy together.

With an **Aries parent** you must beware of too much interference. You like to progress at your own pace, don't you? 1989 rating: there's a special job you must tackle together.

If you have an **Aries child** you can't help trying to restrain him from doing what he wants. Let him follow his own desires. 1989 rating: he or she will approve of your plans.

Your **Aries boy-friend** can be very raw and primitive in some ways! He's a thruster, you're a hugger – so you should manage to have a good time! 1989 rating: torn between duty and pleasure.

An **Aries girl-friend** is very sexy once you've got used to each other. She likes to climb on top, you like a lie-down! 1989 rating: make it an honest relationship.

An **Aries husband** can provide an ideal marriage in lots of ways, so long as you want a real macho man and he wants a cuddly dumpling! 1989 rating: some muddle and deception.

An **Aries wife** will boss you around, but she's fun and full of new ideas. Not a motherly type, though, so it won't be a restful marriage. 1989 rating: someone from her past may turn up,

If your **Aries boss** gives you no peace and quiet, you must leave for another job. 1989 rating: not an unlucky year as such, but you may feel less than perfect together.

Taurus
April 21 to May 21

Friendship Taurean people are among the most gregarious folk in the Zodiac. They love being surrounded by friends, and seek to form firm, solid friendships that last forever. It's part of the deep Taurean need for security. But there's a generous side to the bargain as well. They love plying their friends with food and drink, making them feel at home.

Sex Taurus is one of the sexiest of Zodiac signs. There is a basic earthiness about their approach to sex. They love living in their own bodies and, through kissing and touching, making contact with a loved one's body. They are highly sensual, and the danger is they'll make sex the be-all and end-all of their relationships. If the body loses appeal, they lose interest. A Taurean can too often take the partner's feelings for granted.

Marriage Taureans are made for marriage. It's the most natural way for them to live, sharing with another and building up a strong, mutually supportive family. Ideally they are monogamous by nature, and want to stay faithful. They feel secure within marriage, and would only stray for sexual gratification. Otherwise they make loyal spouses.

Taurus (April 21 to May 21) and You

A relationship resembling the countryside – so settled
it seems it's been there since time began.

Any **Taurus friend** is a solid, reliable pal. Soon, however, life becomes routine between you. There's not enough imagination at times. 1989 rating: there could be some annoying clashes.

A **Taurus parent** will want to live in the past. Because you are younger, you will dislike too much nostalgia. But there are still strong links. 1989 rating: you hear a hard-luck story.

A **Taurus child** will feel you are interfering too much. Do try to live and let live, especially where career is concerned. 1989 rating: good year for enjoying family life together.

A **Taurus boy-friend** is more like a brother than a true lover. You get to know each other too well. Your sex life could become a bit bland. 1989 rating: happy at work, happy at play too.

With a **Taurus girl-friend** you share many attitudes, and enjoy hobbies such as cooking and boozing! A rich, yeasty love affair. 1989 rating: definite optimism in the air.

A **Taurus husband** is the ideal family man – great with children, reliable at bringing home the pay-packet. A bit self-centred. 1989 rating: he'll be planning domestic changes.

A **Taurus wife** is an ideal match for you. You'll grow together like the hills and valleys. You get very set in your ways as you get older. 1989 rating: she could come into money.

With a **Taurus boss** you make a formidable team in business. You see the practical world through the same eyes, and enjoy co-operation together. 1989 rating: you want to keep the peace.

Gemini
May 22 to June 21

Friendship Geminians are the most friendly people in the Zodiac, though, to be honest, they are better at making casual acquaintances than deep personal ties. One reason is that people find them an attractive type, easy to be with, because they have the gift of adapting themselves to suit the company. But they are fair-weather friends. If trouble looms, they don't want to know.

Sex Gemini people talk themselves into and out of love, almost as though it were a game. Gemini is not a highly-sexed sign, even though they may have plenty of sexual experience. Instead, sex for them is a rather special form of conversation. It does not necessarily involve them in deep feelings. But it's quite possible for Geminians to enjoy non-sexual relationships.

Marriage As Gemini is the most devious, two-faced and free-wheeling of all Zodiac signs, it follows that marriage is not really suited to their nature. But they can still make a success of marriage. They need a partner who can keep them on their toes; who can spring surprises; who is more a lover than a spouse; and who, if necessary, can turn a blind eye every time they stray.

Gemini (May 22 to June 21) and You

You provide illuminating insights into each other's character. Gemini seeks variety, while you prefer routine.

A **Gemini friend** is much more restless than you, and you'll have to share him with many other acquaintances. Enjoy this friend while you can. 1989 rating: make a clear-cut plan.

If you have a **Gemini parent** there may be small irritations between you – but on the whole it's a fruitful family link. 1989 rating: there are quarrels that are patched up eventually.

With a **Gemini child** there will be some tantrums to deal

with. Remember that you act as a strong anchor in this child's life. 1989 rating: emotionally you'll feel a bit knocked about.

A **Gemini boy-friend** can be attentive one moment, gone the next! He likes to play games in bed, swopping roles – and partners? 1989 rating: luckily much better now.

A **Gemini girl-friend** is nimble and inventive, and may find you a bit ordinary as a lover. But you've got stamina! Don't rely on her forever. 1989 rating: she'll be changing a lot.

Your **Gemini husband** can be lots of fun but a bit childlike. Don't expect him to be as monogamous as yourself. He likes to flirt. 1989 rating: a sexy year, with more assertiveness.

A **Gemini wife** is the live-wire in the household. She'll keep you busy. If you're a lazy Taurus, she'll look elsewhere for fun. 1989 rating: could be another friendship developing.

If you have a **Gemini boss** he cannot be totally trusted. He'll say one thing and do another. You're his anchor, and he'll rely greatly on you. 1989 rating: concerned about his health.

Cancer
June 22 to July 22

Friendship Cancerians are clannish people at the best of times. They want to be friendly, but they can't help being suspicious of strangers at first. Once they've decided to make someone a friend, they tend to adopt them completely, drawing them into the family, so to speak. Cancerians have a great ability to identify with their friends' feelings, and love sharing.

Sex Although shy at first, Cancer folk soon fall hook, line and sinker for the right sweetheart. They're terrible clingers, hanging on for dear life if a lover seems to be losing interest. Sexually they have access to deep, ecstatic feelings. Physical pleasure is nothing compared with the spiritual orgasms they are capable of experiencing. Cancerians never forget a former sweetheart, and still feel possessive after many years.

Marriage Cancerians are born to be married. They want to share their life with the perfect partner. Cancer men have a good deal of tenderness in their natures; they like strong-minded women who will look after them – indeed, mother them. Cancer women are very feminine, and need men who are kind, loyal and humorous – in short, a homely chap. All Cancerians love their family ties.

Cancer (June 22 to July 22) and You

Both are family types who want to settle down, slowly merging into each other. You're practical, Cancer intuitive.

A **Cancer friend** is the soft type. He or she likes cosy chats, being intimate, sharing inner thoughts. Not sporty, but very clinging. 1989 rating: this could be a special friendship.

With a **Cancer parent** you have many close, almost telepathic ties. In a family crisis you're the ones who stand firm. 1989 rating: there's an underlying anxiety that's not spoken about.

Towards a **Cancer child** you must adopt an encouraging attitude. Too much cuddling will prevent the child from being independent. 1989 rating: a lazy year, when you may neglect each other.

A **Cancer boy-friend** is a cuddler, which you like. But he is moody, and you do like a strong, virile type. His mother is a strong influence. 1989 rating: concentrate on real love.

A **Cancer girl-friend** makes one of the most satisfying Zodiac couples. Together you can make magic in bed. Both of you look towards marriage. 1989 rating: there's a glamorous touch here.

A **Cancer husband** is a perfect marriage partner, so long as you don't marry him too young. Lots of togetherness down the years. 1989 rating: keep a shrewd eye open for deception.

A **Cancer wife** is ideal. Each of you can provide what the other wants: stability, fidelity and a happy home. She has her ups and downs, though. 1989 rating: you'll learn plenty!

If you have a **Cancer boss** you make a reliable partnership in business. 1989 rating: you gain much from each other in 1989. You may be travelling together – with interesting results.

16

Leo
July 23 to August 23

Friendship All Leo folk thrive on friendship, but Leo likes to be the dominant partner. They want to be flattered, praised, loved and enjoyed – that's what friendship means to them. But that isn't all. For a Leo, the heart will always rule the head. They would do anything for a friend – indeed, they put friendship above all.

Sex There's only one thing to do on a hot afternoon – and that is to make love! So think Leo people, anyway. Nothing pleases them more than someone of the opposite sex making eyes at them. They love to be wooed. Falling in love comes very naturally to Leo folk. It's probably true to say that a Leo can't feel truly fulfilled without a good sex life.

Marriage Leos may enjoy flirting at parties, but in the end they are looking for a steady marriage. They need courtship and security at the same time. If ever a marriage breaks up, it can shatter the Leo heart – and like a broken mirror it never quite recovers. A Leo man needs a warmly responsive wife, while the Leo woman wants fidelity and affection.

Leo (July 23 to August 23) **and You**

A relationship producing great passion and less common sense, with great silent rows about nothing at all.

A **Leo friend** can be terrific fun, but may be too fast-moving for you. Beware of being too down-to-earth. Leo always looks for excitement. 1989 rating: a year of glamour and excitement.

If you have a **Leo parent** there could easily be a clash of wills. But you are still seeking the same objectives in life. 1989 rating: another good year. This relationship is blooming.

With a **Leo child** you will also disagree over silly little things; but there's an underlying love for each other. Keep praising each other. 1989 rating: you don't want to be crowded.

With your **Leo boy-friend** once the bonds are formed you'll have a lovely sex life. But he's proud, and hates to be taken for granted. 1989 rating: he'll cut your ideas down to size.

A **Leo girl-friend** expects a lot from you. If you don't live up to her expectations she'll soon ditch you for a real guy. 1989 rating: progress is thwarted by a third party.

Any **Leo husband** wants a tidy home, well-mannered children and a beautifully groomed wife. Can you live up to all that? 1989 rating: you have a small set-back, but can surmount it.

A **Leo wife** is fine, if you have money to burn and entertain a lot. Stuck at home with the kids, she'll feel bored and neglected. 1989 rating: she's taking you too much for granted.

A **Leo boss** is ideal for you. He is good at far-reaching ideas; you enjoy the hard work. 1989 rating: a quarrel could turn into a sulk, exactly what you don't want.

Virgo
August 24 to September 22

Friendship Virgo people distrust strangers. When they meet a new person, they're distant at first. Only when they feel safe will they relax and become more personal. Even then, they are not as friendly as most Zodiac signs. They don't mix as freely, and are much more choosy about friends. They like people who are kindly, intelligent and observant – like themselves.

Sex Traditionally Virgo is the least sexy of all the Zodiac. Virgo people are capable of strong platonic friendships, and they don't seem to need sex as much as other people. Perhaps they need awakening – and once they realize how exciting it can be, they enjoy a splendid sex life. Some Virgoans, particularly women, put themselves on a pedestal, pretending to be far too good for the opposite sex.

Marriage Virgoans tend to remain unmarried longer than other signs. They need space to themselves, where they can be private. Virgoan men need a strong-minded wife who won't be too domineering. He needs someone who will give him enthusiasm as well as encouragement. Virgoan women look for emotional security. They are the kind to have a career outside marriage.

Virgo (August 24 to September 22) and You

Meant to be a good rapport, but there are draw-backs.
You're basically passionate, Virgo more self-contained.

A **Virgo friend** makes an interesting liaison. You share ideas and hobbies in common, but there may not be much warmth. A clever relationship. 1989 rating: not very compatible.

If you have a **Virgo parent** you have a constant worrier, even when there's nothing to worry about. It's hard to get really close to each other. 1989 rating: quite lively and enjoyable.

With a **Virgo child** you may be worried about over-specialization, especially if this child is still at school or college. 1989 rating: can really get to know each other better.

A **Virgo boy-friend** can turn you on in a wonderful way. But is his heart really in it? He will be fussy in little ways. 1989 rating: romance is threatened by silly rows.

A **Virgo girl-friend** is a worrier – about her love life as much as anything. She may be too nervy for your liking. 1989 rating: she may feel threatened by a newcomer.

A **Virgo husband** is not a natural sharer. He will want his own belongings which the family must not interfere with. But an honest, decent man. 1989 rating: havoc in your love life.

A **Virgo wife** will provide a businesslike marriage – the mortgage gets paid, the kids get fed. But she keeps herself to herself. 1989 rating: keep an eye on her spending habits.

A **Virgo boss** will worry about little things, and will make you anxious too. 1989 rating: results may be quite the opposite of what you expect. A topsy-turvy year together.

19

Libra
September 23 to October 23

Friendship Librans thrive on friendship – more than any other Zodiac sign. Without friends they feel lost, only half-alive, for they are so amicable themselves. They mix easily, but can quickly detect if someone is 'not nice'. They adore small talk, chats on the phone, and social gatherings of all kinds. They have the rare ability to stay in touch with childhood friends.

Sex Librans are made for loving! They are one of those Zodiac signs who do distinguish between sex and love. Love without sex is okay, but sex without love is abhorrent. In the right relationship, they want to share themselves, body and soul, with the person they love. They are the psychological type who is drawn to their opposite – not always a good thing!

Marriage Of all Zodiac signs, Libra is the one most suited to marriage. They seem to be born as 'twin souls', and spend their lives looking for the ideal mate. Librans of both sexes need someone who is a good pal as well as lover. Libran men need an organized woman who isn't bossy. Libran women feel they need a real macho man who will look after them forever.

Libra (September 23 to October 23) **and You**

Both are ruled by Venus, so plenty of affection.
You like being sociable at home, Libra enjoys visiting.

Any **Libra friend** is a lovely companion, and you can be pals for life. Neither of you is looking for an argument. Great for artistic interests. 1989 rating: a pleasant year.

With a **Libra parent** you have a solid admirer all your life. Even though you're different people, you share similar tastes. 1989 rating: a happy year in the family circle.

If you have a **Libra child** you should have a sweet relationship. You are both artistic, keen on the beautiful side of life. 1989 rating: will delight older relatives.

A **Libra boy-friend** is gentle and considerate, and will treasure you. You'll be the one who makes the decisions, though. 1989 rating: quite a happy year, with luck in the summer.

A **Libra girl-friend** makes a wonderful match with you. She wants you to take the lead. If you show her how, she'll do anything you want. 1989 rating: terrific for a reconciliation.

With a **Libra husband** you make a lovely couple. He'll do exactly what you want – though he's not very handy with practical chores. 1989 rating: after a dull start, much more lively.

A **Libra wife** is nice and jolly. You're charming to each other, provided you don't get too selfish. You're both good with children, nice to neighbours. 1989 rating: events in your favour.

With a **Libra boss** you get your own way if you stay dogged. He will be persuaded by your ideas. 1989 rating: a holiday apart does you the world of good.

Scorpio
October 24 to November 22

Friendship Scorpio people are highly suspicious of newcomers. They don't make friends easily, and they can test their friendships so severely that they frighten would-be pals away. But once a true friendship is formed, it lasts for life. As far as Scorpio is concerned, friendship is a matter of utter loyalty. Friendship with members of their own sex is very important.

Sex Sex is a deeper, richer experience for Scorpio than perhaps for anyone else. At the same time, they manage to make sex far more complex and meaningful than it need be. Many Scorpians are frightened of sexual power. Raw sex, without love, worries them more than most people. It's certainly hard for them to have a casual, lightweight affair. As in so many other aspects of their lives, it's all or nothing.

Marriage Scorpians don't take their marriage vows lightly.

21

They mean to keep them, through bad times as well as good. They can be very jealous if slighted, but within a happy relationship they are the happiest of partners, for they are capable of much devotion. Scorpio men need a woman who can be a real soul-mate. Scorpio women need a strong man – the tougher the better.

Scorpio (October 24 to November 22) and You

A great love-hate relationship. Can be tremendously warm but you can both wonder why you ever came together!

A **Scorpio friend** is a complex creature and will want you to prove your friendship in some way. But you've a lot going for you. 1989 rating: could play a bit part in your life.

With a **Scorpio parent** you have deep, intense links, for better or worse. Sometimes you feel chained together. Not easy to forget this influence. 1989 rating: tries to manipulate you.

The same applies to a **Scorpio child,** who tends to cling to you. You make a marvellous team, so long as you don't start hating each other! 1989 rating: there's a nice holiday atmosphere.

A **Scorpio boy-friend** is the sort of man you can become obsessed by. He's fascinating, strong-willed and possessive. 1989 rating: try to keep him happy.

You and a **Scorpio girl-friend** make one of the sexiest combinations in the Zodiac. She has a rich, sensuous nature that exactly suits yours. 1989 rating: your love life gets interesting.

With a **Scorpio husband** you're letting yourself into a testing marriage. He wants all or nothing – so make sure you deliver it! 1989 rating: good links, but you may feel insecure.

A **Scorpio wife** provides a till-death-us-do-part marriage. You'll cling to each other, through bad times and good, or glower silently! 1989 rating: a pleasant year together, with good news.

A **Scorpio boss** will take out his troubles on you. But he enjoys a crisis, and is reliable. 1989 rating: do a favour, and you'll be happily rewarded.

Sagittarius
November 23 to December 21

Friendship Sagittarians are friendly – for a while – but people cannot rely on them. They can drop friends as easily as they can pick them up – without much heartbreak. Most Sagittarians have a built-in charm that never fails to attract. There's a relaxed, informal manner which doesn't really look for lasting links. They like new people, so old pals are taken for granted.

Sex They have a very flirtatious manner that enjoys chatting up the opposite sex. There's also an element of victory involved. They like to win hearts, and at times they get a thrill from leaving a broken heart by the wayside. Sagittarians enjoy sex on impulse, perhaps in exotic locations! They can get bored with the sameness of love-making with the same old partner!

Marriage Sagittarians are not the most monogamous of people. It's hard for them to maintain interest in one person all their lives. So they need partners who have the same variety-seeking outlook on life that Sagittarians have. Men born under Sagittarius appreciate a woman with a mind of her own. Sagittarian women respond to real men, full of zest for life.

Sagittarius (November 23 to December 21) **and You**

Not much in common. Sagittarius wants to roam the world while you like to stay put. So lots of crossed wires!

A **Sagittarius friend** will tease you, quarrel with you, drag you off on trips – but if you don't respond, he'll get bored. 1989 rating: plenty to do together.

With a **Sagittarius parent** you have a jolly, carefree Mum or Dad. It's a robust relationship standing the test of time. 1989 rating: you're tempted to be rebellious.

With a **Sagittarius child** you have a right little tearabout on your hands. Life will be full of fun, though. Expect him or her to leave home early. 1989 rating: may get into trouble.

A **Sagittarius boy-friend** is much more free-and-easy than yourself. He'll adore seducing you, but while you like sexual routine, he likes variety. 1989 rating: a marvellous year.

A **Sagittarius girl-friend** gets this relationship off to a flying start, but she needs a varied sexual diet. If you get jealous, she'll shrug and leave. 1989 rating: have a wonderful time.

A **Sagittarius husband** will love having you as his little woman at home – someone he returns to after his male adventures. 1989 rating: a lively year, except for one incident.

A **Sagittarius wife** will keep you on your toes. If you don't liven up, she'll pack her bags. Don't think she's just a housewife. 1989 rating: you talk a lot, and get little done!

A **Sagittarius boss** is full of well-meaning ideas, but has he the force of character you like? 1989 rating: a difficult year, so that it feels like a bad marriage!

Capricorn
December 22 to January 20

Friendship Capricorn folk make friends with difficulty – but once made, they tend to remain friends for life. The wall around the Capricorn heart makes it hard for us to get to know them well. Friendship for the Capricorn type is not a light-hearted, take-it-or-leave-it affair. It must be based on real virtues such as trust, honour and the readiness to help.

Sex Capricorn people have such a cold manner at times that they appear unsexy. Actually they are highly sexed, though it does not always flow out in a harmonious way. They are not flirty types. They adopt a serious approach to life, and can turn nasty and jealous if slighted. Yet their planet Saturn is linked to the old Roman orgies, so they can certainly let themselves go! They can turn from frost to warmth in a split second!

Marriage Marriage is a solemn matter to Capricorn folk. They intend to make it last for life. Once married, they feel they own their partners. They don't look for freedom or adventure. All their energies are devoted to maintaining the marriage as it is. This can lead to a stale situation where they take their spouses too much for granted.

Capricorn (December 22 to January 20) and You

An admirable, strong and capable combination,
though you may not like each other straight away.

A **Capricorn friend** respects you, as you both see the world through similar eyes. Very businesslike and capable, though you can depress each other! 1989 rating: disappointing.

A **Capricorn parent** is a serious-minded person who will have given you a solid upbringing. You can be too gloomy together. 1989 rating: little touches make all the difference.

A **Capricorn child** is steady, willing, a bit quiet and not as extrovert as yourself. But others will say you're so alike! 1989 rating: his laziness will make you mad.

A **Capricorn boy-friend** is a puritan at heart. Your earthy approach to sex will warm him up – eventually! He's a very self-contained chap. 1989 rating: an amiable year together.

A **Capricorn girl-friend** is a slow starter, but once you're lovers she'll prove a worthwhile partner. This can be a very physical affair. 1989 rating: do what you're told!

A **Capricorn husband** suits you nicely. This is a sensible marriage, based on respect and common sense. But you must keep in touch – literally! 1989 rating: his health could suffer.

A **Capricorn wife** makes a fine marriage partner. This union should grow richer and steadier as the years go by. You can build a great life together. 1989 rating: someone else wants her.

A **Capricorn boss**, meanwhile, can work admirably with you. You make a good team, especially in engineering. 1989 rating: a lovely working year together – and the friendship improves.

Aquarius
January 21 to February 18

Friendship Friendships mean much to Aquarians. At the same time they want to remain independent. So they are friendly with lots of people, but always slightly stand-offish – as if they are really on their own. Aquarians are good at making and keeping friends. Primarily they are interested in mental friendship – the rapport between people who share the same interests.

Sex Aquarius is one of three signs (Gemini and Virgo are the others) that are not obviously sexual. Don't worry, they can have a perfectly normal and happy love life; but they treat people as humans first, and as sexual partners only later. They are capable of great tenderness. But a passionate partner will say they don't get sufficiently involved.

Marriage Aquarians see their partners as equals – not people who must be dominated or obeyed. At the same time they're freedom-loving in outlook, so it's difficult for them to share the little things in life. They need emotional elbow-room, and hate to be owned or trapped. Aquarians are rarely the unhappy victims of marriage. If it breaks up, Aquarians are the first to go.

Aquarius (January 21 to February 18) and You

Aquarius is a natural radical, while you are a conservative.
There needs to be tolerance in this relationship.

An **Aquarius friend** is stimulating at a mental level, but not as down-to-earth as you. He hates routine – you love it! 1989 rating: you must cheer each other up.

An **Aquarius parent** gave you a free-and-easy upbringing. Don't expect him or her to molly-coddle you now. There should be mutual respect on both sides. 1989 rating: be generous.

26

With an **Aquarius child** you are too clinging by half. You must respect this child's privacy, and allow plenty of freedom. 1989 rating: nice year to try something new together.

An **Aquarius boy-friend** doesn't get as involved in sex as you do. You must be full of tricks to keep him interested. 1989 rating: a special holiday makes all the difference.

An **Aquarius girl-friend** is not really compatible. She's a thinker, you're a feeler. Sex in the head for her versus sex in the body for you. 1989 rating: a small tiff could grow into a big quarrel.

An **Aquarius husband** has his head in the clouds, while your feet are on the ground. So you can be an idealistic yet stable match. 1989 rating: it's easy for you to give in.

An **Aquarius wife** is a bit too independent for your liking. She's lively, bright but a bit odd, and doesn't much enjoy housework. 1989 rating: someone else provides a surprise.

If you have an **Aquarius boss** you work well, but can be stubborn over details. 1989 rating: financially you do well, and you're going places together.

Pisces
February 19 to March 20

Friendship Pisceans are friendly folk. They enjoy meeting new people and can quickly become dependent on new friends – for love, loyalty and, if need be, support if things go wrong. At the same time they don't like to be 'owned', and get frustrated if chums try to organize their lives too much. Piscean men relate well to women, but Piscean women may be in awe of clever male friends.

Sex The Piscean aim in love is to achieve a wonderful, yielding rapport with their partners. They want to melt into love-making, losing their own identity. All the same, Pisceans are fussy in choosing the right partner. Because their imagination is powerful, they can see a would-be sexual partner in a rosy-coloured light, and can be terribly let down later. Sex without love does not suit the Piscean at all.

Marriage Pisceans have an ambiguous attitude towards marriage. In one way, their whole impulse is to make someone else happy and fulfilled. At the same time, they need to feel free. They should not marry someone who will be too possessive. Piscean men look for a woman who will take the lead in the marriage. Piscean women can be misused by an over-dominant husband.

Pisces (February 19 to March 20) and You

These two different temperaments can achieve a real rapport.
Dreamy Pisces is a nice antidote to practical Taurus.

A **Pisces friend** is quirky and good-humoured, and a good deal more emotional and unstable than you. You're the anchor in this relationship. 1989 rating: saying goodbye?

A **Pisces parent** will have neglected you or smothered you in love. You are a good deal more practical and steady, and have the stronger personality. 1989 rating: there are hopeful signs.

A **Pisces child** is a slippery creature, full of love one moment and white lies the next! You are quite telepathic together. 1989 rating: a lively year, enjoy your holidays.

A **Pisces boy-friend** is more deeply involved than he likes to let on. He's a tricky customer, and not always reliable. 1989 rating: a row lasts a long time, so avoid it if possible.

A **Pisces girl-friend** will think of you as a real man. So long as you stay romantic, she'll love you for ever. She sees you through rose-coloured specs. 1989 rating: lots of excitement.

A **Pisces husband** is not very ambitious, or may make a mess of his career. But his heart's in the right place. Try not to be too predictable. 1989 rating: rather a moody year.

A **Pisces wife** can be untidy, scatter-brained, but full of good intentions. She's great with children and pets, but keep the drink away from her! 1989 rating: good year.

From a **Pisces boss** you get promises, hopes, dreams – but precious little reality! 1989 rating: you want to get close to each other, and not just in business.

Your Birthday Message

*This book applies to everyone born between
April 21 and May 21. But here, just for you,
is a special word of hope or caution,
depending on your actual birthday in Taurus.
Here is your own astrological message
to guide you through the year ahead.*

APRIL

Friday 21st: A lively and versatile year. You will move into a new circle of friends. A friend may be curious about your private life, and create trouble. Best month: July.

Saturday 22nd: A serious, hard-working year. There won't be much leisure time. There could be back trouble, despite – or because of – a lot of lively romance.

Sunday 23rd: Daydreams get you nowhere. You must egg on a pal to be braver and bolder, or you'll get nowhere together. A good year to start a new business commitment.

Monday 24th: You gain what you want – little by little. If you are too greedy, it could all slip away. Not an easy year for handling money. Have fun with a new sweetheart.

Tuesday 25th: Still a good year for you, with a lot of brand-new activities in your life. Beware of trying to do things too quickly. Very lucky in the early summer.

Wednesday 26th: There could be a make-or-break phase in a marriage or love affair. I think love triumphs in the end. You will get more into debt, but you'll also earn more.

Thursday 27th: A sweet-natured year. Religion or the paranormal could play a significant role in your life. There is some embarrassment in your emotional life, but you remain popular.

Friday 28th: A year of fizz and sparkle. You'll make some new friends, plus one or two enemies. You can't win 'em all! A year for kicking over the traces.

Saturday 29th: A cheerful, good-humoured year. If you make extra money, you'll soon spend it. Live for today is your motto. Excellent year for romance, the more the merrier!

Sunday 30th: A sudden change will create a golden opportunity. Think twice before saying 'yes' – you won't be sorry. Don't lend money to someone who is deceiving you.

MAY

Monday 1st: There are extra responsibilities, but don't let them make you too gloomy. Enjoy the lighter side of life, too. Beware of innocently breaking the law.

Tuesday 2nd: Your life is moving into a serious phase. It'll be a hard-working, ambitious time for you. Tit for tat should be your motto. Elderly relatives need a helping hand.

Wednesday 3rd: Excellent if you use your brain in a creative way. In business and finance you could make a sudden advance. Romance is more problematic.

Thursday 4th: You can get bogged down by a silly episode. Try to put it quickly behind you. Clear your mind of trivia, and be prepared to make domestic changes.

Friday 5th: A serene year – except for one disappointment – perhaps in love, perhaps in finance. Think things out – before rushing in! You may be in other people's hands, all the same.

Saturday 6th: Some mental stress, perhaps from someone who should be loyal to you. Grasp an exciting opportunity quickly. An enjoyable year, with people suddenly on your side.

Sunday 7th: Some surprises in store, so you'll be kept on your toes this year. A sudden friendship comes and goes. A new leisure pursuit really thrills you, and proves obsessive.

Monday 8th: You're clinging to the past too much. Prune out the dead wood, and you'll soon start blossoming again. Nice financial opportunities in mid-summer, but problems at year's end.

Tuesday 9th: Take a small risk by all means. A whopping change in life will bring you back to square one, though. There's a secret in the family circle that needs digging out.

Wednesday 10th: You could gamble too much. A child will go his own way. You must keep your emotional life under control, or there may be nothing left.

Thursday 11th: A risk-taking, slightly accident-prone year, due to over-hastiness on your part. Always keep your eye on long-term objectives, and don't worry over health.

Friday 12th: Your cosy Taurus niche is going to be disturbed. Don't worry, it may do you good – but be awkward for a while. You do well in competitions and contests.

Saturday 13th: A risky year, but with a good chance of success. There's more freedom of action in your life. Excellent year for asking favours, and having them granted.

Sunday 14th: You will keep your nerve in a crisis. Excellent time for taking a serious decision – in work or love. There could be family squabbles, and travel is favoured.

Monday 15th: Things go well. You could get deeper into a relationship that you don't know will really work out. There may be retraining at work. There could be an accident to arm or leg.

Tuesday 16th: Someone tries to be too inquisitive about your private life. Quite an old-fashioned year – you'll be fed up with people who try to be too modern.

Wednesday 17th: You feel happier, but there's a possible cloud on the horizon. Beware of going to law; you may not end up the winner. Someone could disappear out of your life in 1989.

Thursday 18th: A crucial time in your life when you may discover what it's all about. Beware of a chip on your shoulder spoiling the outlook for you. Lots of mental rapport with one person.

Friday 19th: At work you'll benefit from a new scheme. Quite a lot of fun, especially on an overseas holiday, but you still don't feel entirely in charge of your own life.

Saturday 20th: An unpleasant phase of life is coming to an end. A good year for you, with progress on several fronts. Someone young and beautiful may lead you astray!

Sunday 21st: You'll do well in 1989. A new career may beckon, and your love life looks more secure and happy. One problem may concern your health. Family life is terrific.

Your Year Ahead

If there were tensions in an existing relationship in late 1988, these should be resolved, one way or another, in the New Year. 1989 appears to be the year when you turn over a new leaf. There's an air of expectancy and genuine optimism.

January could bring old friends nearer. Your social life will be interesting and full. February will be difficult, with a number of small, irritating problems to cope with.

March seems much better, and brings a career-orientated phase of life. The company you work for could be in trouble, and you must make a big effort to save your employment.

Easter marks a watershed in some way. You'll really be enthusiastic about the future. Someone who entered your life last year, then disappeared, may come back, but in changed circumstances.

Watch out for a possible accident in May, but June looks lucky and pleasant, especially if you're a gardener. You may be caught between conscience and desire – and in the end will take caution rather than risking actions.

July is full of family life with a clash between the generations likely, though not seriously so. In August or September there will be thoughts of moving house, or redecorations. August looks highly sociable, and September sees the start of the educational year, when you could well be following a course of study.

October could find some bad luck, though you recover quickly. November could find you poorly, while December finds other relatives ill.

Basically things do look better by the end of 1989, and there will be plenty to look forward to in the 1990s. In particular, romance and finance are both looking better, while a career pattern may change – but basically for the better.

New-born Taurus children face a trouble-free 1989. The only danger could come from whooping cough or a similar respiratory complaint. They are bright and observant infants who won't want to linger with mother for too long. They're too independent.

Taurus **youngsters** face a challenging year. They may have to grow up quicker than they want. They do well in exams, but only after a last-minute panic!

Elderly Taurus people have quite a lot of illness, especially heart trouble or high blood pressure. It needn't be serious, but you'll have to take things easy. So you won't be so mobile, but life is otherwise quite enjoyable.

If you are **chronically ill** there is unlikely to be a drastic new treatment to relieve symptoms. With a bit of luck, however, things will put themselves right. There's a real chance that disease will simply vanish.

Out-of-work Taurus folk have two excellent chances of finding the right job this coming year: the first is February-March, the second is mid-1989. You need a job where you can use your charm and sociability.

If you **run your own business** you must face the possibility of a down-turn in trade in the first six months, with a fine recovery period thereafter. If you want to start your own business, I suggest you start in the second half of the year.

If the last few months – or years – have been **lonely**, you have a wonderful chance early in 1989 to find a new lover. You may not be able to keep him or her, though – sorry about that!

Taurus people who have a **rocky marriage** may decide that 1989 is the year to end it. This could lead to a time of some emptiness, and for some Taureans there will be a reconciliation in the final months of the year.

If you are planning to **move** the signs are good that the change will be beneficial for all concerned. A removal overseas is specially favoured. Even if you are not looking forward to such a change, it will be much better than expected.

January
Guide

You seem in a lively, self-satisfied frame of mind for much of the month. Normally your type of Taurean personality is gentle and tolerant, but this month you are more ambitious and driven then usual.

Everyone knows that you are stubborn, and this month you'll cling to a pre-conceived idea. People will find you surprisingly determined though you prefer to see yourself as strong-minded.

It's certainly a time when you want to look back to the past, not perhaps the recent past, but several years ago. You may feel that history is about to repeat itself.

Two words of warning: don't be taken in by surface appearances, but try to let your intuition tell you whether a person is good or bad, and do try to forgive and forget.

WORK. A couple of nice things happen this month. You get on well with the boss, and if you are thinking of changing jobs your would-be employer seems really nice.

If you're self-employed, you have a number of new jobs this month, including one customer who will become a favourite.

It's a great time for interviews and around-the-table discussions, and there should be a spirit of enterprise and co-operation between labour and management.

Possibly an event at home will have consequences on your working life. You may have to get special permission.

HOME. A spot of carelessness at home could lead to a narrow miss. Don't leave food cooking by itself, and put all fires out when a room's not in use.

The place may be livelier than usual, especially with teenagers present, and there may be a disturbance in your street – through road works or perhaps a diversion.

For some Taureans it's the right time to think about moving house or to change your living arrangements.

If you are hard up, you'll receive help for the family from an unexpected quarter.

HEALTH. It's the right time to have your teeth checked – especially if you haven't been for some time.

You are more prone than usual to odd winter infections, especially if your eating habits or sleeping hours are disturbed. And you can help yourself and others to take better care. A campaign in your district could bring home the importance of preventative medicine.

MONEY. It's a good month to raise money for charity, or to get a sizeable loan for yourself, whether for business or family.

An investment to watch is a local company that's suddenly on the up and up. If you are offered shares in the company you work for, it's a good idea to accept them – and maybe buy more. You could be on to a winner this year.

As far as gambling is concerned, racing's really cut short by bad weather, but if you chose carefully – especially third and fourth favourites – you could get a number of winners.

LEISURE. It's a month when you'll enjoy putting your feet up, especially if you had a busy Christmas and New Year.

You'll enjoy getting friends together for a special purpose – perhaps to form a new committee, leisure group or hobbyists' club. Whatever the reason, use a touch of originality.

It's a good month to make the most of your personal charm. You could have a couple of glamorous evenings out, and you should be more popular than usual.

If you help to run a club, your skills will be more needed than ever. If other people start acting strangely, you're the one to pull them back to the straight and narrow.

LOVE. You may have some difficulty in handling your partner's moods, especially if he or she is a Cancer or Scorpio type.

You're feeling quite eager and ardent, especially if a new relationship is in the offing. You'll enjoy taking the lead, and will want to make sure you're going steady. Unfortunately the would-be sweetheart wants to keep things free and easy.

January
Key Dates

Sunday 1st: *Slightly argumentative, but happy on the whole. Family squabbles, perhaps.* Tuesday looks irritable, and you may lose your temper.

Monday 2nd: *Exciting, but beware of blowing a fuse. You could lose your temper.* Make sure everything is locked, if leaving the house – and lock the car at all times.

Tuesday 3rd: *Slightly rougher. Good day for driving yourself hard.* You should be involved with charity work. Something comes to the end of its useful life.

Wednesday 4th: *Still a difficult time. Expect an explosion of rage, but one bit of luck, too.* Look forward to some good news on the personal front.

Thursday 5th: *A puzzling day, with people behaving in an inconsistent fashion.* You'll be roused from laziness by a surprise event. Lucky numbers: 4, 7.

Friday 6th: *Friendly time, with the accent on getting to know people better.* A relative might not be pleased to see you. You may be getting fed up with your usual friends.

Saturday 7th: *Not an organized day, but plenty gets done. A time to enjoy yourself.* Your partner will be independent-minded. There needn't be a row – just silent frustration.

Sunday 8th: *Smoothly flowing day. Lots will be packed into the time available.* Attend to a minor health complaint before it gets worse. Think about gardening for the summer.

Monday 9th: *Travel plans run into difficulties. People are not easy-going.* Someone with the initial H or N could help you. Problems at work, especially if people don't turn up.

Tuesday 10th: *Lots of optimism, keeping your fingers crossed, and hoping for the best.* A cold caught now will linger for a long time. Try to put a stop to it.

Wednesday 11th: *An ideal family time. People should feel close and affectionate.* There could be trouble with plumbing. You say goodbye eventually, but people outstay their welcome.

Thursday 12th: *A practical day when solutions can be found to* *any problem.* Someone younger than yourself will be a help. Lucky colour: pink, black.

Friday 13th: *Accident-prone time. Something smoothly-running could go wrong.* Your working week will be a strain. You'll be glad to get home for the weekend.

Saturday 14th: *A careful, painstaking day – but there may still be a surprise.* You have contact with someone from another part of the country.

Sunday 15th: *You must act wisely, out of the best of motives. A sensitive day for money.* There's a mystery in your life. Perhaps something disappears, or news is kept from you.

Monday 16th: *Very energetic and self-confident, with plenty of luck operating.* At home there's a cosy evening in store. Terrific for young lovers – and old ones, too!

Tuesday 17th: *Romantic, life-loving and still lucky – so make the most of it!* The accent is on co-operation and friendship. Don't be swayed by someone who's out to make mischief.

Wednesday 18th: *An inventive day. Someone may throw a friendly spanner in the works.* You can reach a friendly understanding with a would-be friend, but don't take it too far too soon.

Thursday 19th: *Slight air of melancholy, also a snappy mood at times.* A trip to a museum or stately home will be interesting but expensive. You could be lucky this afternoon.

Friday 20th: *A struggle for power – subtly, not with force. Family affairs important.* Certainly a friendly day. Even a bully will be pleasant to you!

Saturday 21st: *Muddled day, nothing settled. Touch of violence in the air.* This is a slightly unrealistic time for you. Promises won't be quickly fulfilled, so you must bide your time.

Sunday 22nd: *There's a return to the past, but a desire for new action.* There'll be a hunt for a lost object, which you may never see again. You have a good laugh this evening.

Monday 23rd: *Imagination gets wild and woolly. Good for creative work.* Learn something new; you'll soon see the value of it. Help is at hand, if you need it. Do ask.

Tuesday 24th: *More optimistic. It's time to deal with an out-of-date organization.* If you've recently had a shock, take life easy. See life from someone else's viewpoint.

Wednesday 25th: *Free-wheeling sort of day. Happiness could burst out of nowhere.* A repair will cost more than you bargained for. There may be an unexpected visitor.

Thursday 26th: *At a practical level, plenty can be achieved. In personal life, still warm-hearted.* A health problem could cost you money. Great for outdoor hobbies – or sport.

Friday 27th: *A time when middle-aged people do better than youngsters.* You will succeed where everyone said you'd fail. Lucky numbers: 2, 10. Lucky colours: white, scarlet.

Saturday 28th: *Very lucky day for some people. A blessing comes out of the blue.* A domestic gadget could go haywire. Even if there are problems, you'll laugh them off.

Sunday 29th: *Cheerful day when people exaggerate. Good for a party or other get-together.* Rather a bloody-minded time. People will obstruct you. Maybe you need more privacy.

Monday 30th: *Much better. A lot of luck and happiness for many people today.* Muscles will get tired if you work too hard. Give extra work to others, if possible.

Tuesday 31st: *Time to put the past behind you. Don't let a nasty feeling obsess you.* Make sure your clothes fit properly – especially shoes. Keep a sense of humour.

Wise Words for January

Odd things animals.
All dogs look up to you. All cats look down on you.
Only a pig looks at you as an equal.
Winston Churchill.

38

February
Guide

The start of February seems a difficult time, and the rest of the month depends on a decision that's made at the end of the first week.

With a bit of luck everything will be sorted out, leaving you to enjoy life in a relatively uncluttered way. However, things could become more complicated still, tying your hands in a way you don't like.

Home life seems particularly fraught, perhaps involving a clash between the generations or between husband and wife.

There's luck for Taureans involved in sales – whether in business or your private life.

WORK. There will be arguments at work this month, but you must seek reconciliation rather than aggravation. If you're the type who changes job quite often, I can see a further move this month – especially into something slightly glamorous like fashion, the beauty industry, advertising or market research.

If there's a crisis for you in early February, it could be that you are being hurried in a direction you are uncertain about. Take your time, and then you'll make the right choice.

Some Taureans could be involved in a big re-organization at your work place. You won't want to stand out from the crowd, but will prefer to go along with the wishes of others.

HOME. You may play a role in a child's education, getting involved in the local school, or perhaps having a stand-up row with a teacher over your child's progress.

Household expenses will increase, perhaps thanks to a new gadget or system at home that eats up extra money. Still, it will be much more comfortable and convenient, so it's worthwhile in the long run.

HEALTH. If you suffer from high blood pressure, there could be a bad couple of weeks in February. And if you are prone to arthritis, joints may be particularly swollen for a while.

If you are introduced to a new drug, it could be having

unpleasant side-effects, though these will diminish in a few weeks' time.

MONEY. It's a good time to sort out a better budget for yourself, spending less on trivialities and more, hopefully, on a hobby that really interests you.

If you are saving towards a major purchase – like a new car – you must stick to your savings plan or you won't get the thing in time.

It looks as though there could be a better deal on housing – a reduction in the mortgage rate, for instance, or the minimum deposit required for a house.

The Stock Market could be moving down this month, so you'll want to sell in the first week unless you want to avoid a loss.

If you're a gambler, there could be some luck on the football pools, especially if you're part of a pools syndicate.

LEISURE. You are in an artistic frame of mind, and will enjoy concentrating on an art-form, be it painting, writing, music or whatever. You will benefit from a bit of experienced coaching, so don't be too proud to ask for it.

In your social life you need to stay in the swim of things, especially if you see a friend moving into a new social group. It's a nice month for a group outing, joining a new club and perhaps joining up with others through correspondence or a computer link.

LOVE. No one budges your heart very quickly, but this month you are more flirtatious than usual. There could be a crunch in your love life in the first week, and depending on that outcome you will either be much happier with the person concerned – or looking for someone new.

There could be a small cloud hanging over one personal friendship. It could be a separation has to be endured, or maybe there's just a temporary lack of communication. You could be flirting with one person, but still feeling loyal to someone else.

You get on best with Libra, worst with Leo.

February
Key Dates

Wednesday 1st: *Nothing goes quite to plan. The bright ideas are still favoured.* Use a friendship to sort out a dispute. You can help people in return.

Thursday 2nd: *A calming influence. The rough and tumble of the last few days gives way to peace.* Legal matters will move ahead. You'll feel happier, and more hopeful.

Friday 3rd: *Still a gentle time. People should co-operate with each other.* A muddle over dates brings a disappointment. Never mind, you have plenty to do on your own.

Saturday 4th: *There's a new initiative. Expect a sudden breakthrough.* Go easy with drink, as it will rush to your head today! A party may get on your nerves.

Sunday 5th: *The middle of a really lucky phase. The tide should flow in your favour.* A phone call out of the blue will set your mind buzzing with ideas.

Monday 6th: *A lucky day for many, but high hopes could be dashed.* Good week to deal with organizations. A second or third attempt is well worthwhile – keep on trying!

Tuesday 7th: *Fantastic day for happy-go-lucky travel and trying something out-of-the-ordinary.* Someone may suggest that you go into business together, if only in a part-time way.

Wednesday 8th: *Lots of warmth and fellow-feeling. Ideal time to meet someone you fancy.* Socially you may feel left out, perhaps because you were slow to say 'yes'.

Thursday 9th: *Someone tries something new. A surprising day in many ways.* It is a day of high passions, with tempers flying. You get on well with Gemini and Sagittarius.

Friday 10th: *Oddball day. You'll want to get out of a rut, and do something different.* Slimming is an uphill battle today. You'll feel like tucking into your grub!

Saturday 11th: *Something could be snatched away at the last moment.* You should spend time with a sensitive person who is in tune with you. Lucky numbers: 3, 6.

Sunday 12th: *People – or belongings – get lost. An escapist* *weekend for many.* You may be caught between two people, and not know which way to turn.

Monday 13th: *Lovely, zippy day, ideal for moving around and travelling.* If you share your home with others, there could soon be a new arrival. Enjoy people – don't be so critical.

Tuesday 14th: *A day of surprises. You can talk your way out of difficulties.* You run the risk of catching a contagious complaint from someone close to you.

Wednesday 15th: *A thrifty day. You won't be able to do what you want.* Good day for selling something. You must reach a decision affecting others.

Thursday 16th: *Someone will keep you guessing. Lots of passion on the boil.* Be cautious about buying something expensive. You need more time before committing yourself – to anything.

Friday 17th: *Quite a daring time. Something dangerous will be successfully accomplished.* Illness could upset your plans. Keep at something – persistence pays off.

Saturday 18th: *A fun day, with plenty happening. You'll want to get away from reality.* A positive weekend. You can cheer up someone in distress. An unexpected offer leads to happiness

Sunday 19th: *Another loving day when everyone gets on well with each other.* It's a busy time as far as the family is concerned. Someone gets angry, so calm them down.

Monday 20th: *You'll be happy to bid farewell to a state of affairs. It's a new beginning.* An evening out means you'll bump into an old friend. Life at work is a real bore.

Tuesday 21st: *Quite cheerful. A day for getting plenty done, either face to face or on the phone.* You feel like stepping out of line, whatever others may say.

Wednesday 22nd: *Not a stable, steady time. Good day for thinking about the future.* At work you can earn good marks. A great time for taking exams. Have confidence in yourself.

Thursday 23rd: *Peaceful, quiet day, except some men want to rock the boat.* There will be a favourable response if you have a favour to ask. Have fun with a new lover.

Friday 24th: *Warmth slips out of a relationship. Many people appear self-centred.* You may have to help a neighbour look after himself. Parental influence will be ignored.

Saturday 25th: *There may be a mild backlash from mean-minded folk.* Be careful around the home – a careless mistake could lead to real trouble. Lucky initials: R or T.

Sunday 26th: *A trusting-to-luck day. Things could turn out very nicely.* An energetic Saturday followed by a restful Sunday. Put your feet up, and get plenty of sleep.

Monday 27th: *Quite cheerful in the circumstances. Basically a loving, supportive day.* You could be praised for a practical achievement. Maybe you're lucky, too.

Tuesday 28th: *A more amiable time when people want to relax in a spot of fantasy.* Don't be taken for granted. You may have to shout to make yourself heard.

Wise Words for February

Insanity is hereditary.
You get it from your kids.
Badge

March
Guide

Your mood should be brighter, even though a decision you've been waiting for may leave you hanging in the air. You'll get some real help from an older person, especially if you're planning something new in education or business over the next few years.

There's a puzzling time in later March, however, with an air of amiable muddle hanging over your life. Don't be surprised if there are missed chances, unpunctual meetings or last-minute changes of plan. Someone is keeping a secret from you.

All the same, you stay confident, with a nice appetite for life. There's good news from abroad, especially if you already have friends or family overseas.

WORK. You may still be plotting and planning changes in your life, without anything definite happening. You may have to accept more responsibility, due to illness or holidays, and there's one good chance of impressing a superior, and perhaps earning yourself some promotion in the future.

You may be called upon to practise a skill you haven't done for years, but it all comes back to you quickly enough.

Around mid-March there could be a bonus coming your way, and it's an excellent time for helping someone else improve his or her career chances.

HOME. They may not make it obvious, but people will be grateful to you as a source of strength and stability in the household. There may even be some upheaval in the neighbourhood in which you'll play a part to calm things down.

This could be a local issue which you will raise with a councillor or government official, or there may be a complaint raised by a neighbour.

Among the family itself there is a buoyant atmosphere, with one child doing particularly well. If you share a flat with friends, there may be one sad departure and another interesting arrival.

HEALTH. If you suffer from a chronic illness, it has a good chance now to lessen its effect on you. Comparatively speaking, you should feel as fit as a fiddle.

Some minor complaint that you've always treated yourself, not very successfully, may now have a much more effective medical cure – so don't hesitate to see your doctor about it.

The only real health problem this month could be accident-proneness in the second half, though perhaps you may unwittingly cause someone else to have a mishap rather than you yourself.

MONEY. You continue to be lucky in the first ten days, whether in the football pools, racing or the Stock Market. Although the general budget news may not suit you, there will be one item that applies directly to you.

If you have savings to invest, watch out for a new privatization scheme on which you can double your money.

You may have to worry about someone else's financial affairs for a while. A child or partner could have been extravagant and landed in a mess. You can handle it, but it's a nuisance.

LEISURE. You will have a good time taking part in an amateur or professional performance, and enjoy the sound of applause ringing in your ears.

But you can't do entirely your own thing, as family duty may keep you at home more than you would wish.

It's a good time to be entering a competition, and doing much better than you expected.

You will also enjoy a group activity, especially if it will culminate in a performance.

LOVE. For some Taureans romance will be a bit fluid this month, so you aren't sure of your own feelings. To some extent you may feel trapped by someone else's strong feelings.

If you have got more than one sweetheart, you may feel that one of them is manipulating you to give up the other. This you don't want to do, so it's the time to start telling white lies.

You get on well with Virgo and Capricorn folk this month, though less happily with Cancer and Scorpio.

March
Key Dates

Wednesday 1st: *Good day for family affairs – almost telepathic rapport.* At home there could be some trouble, involving extra expense.

Thursday 2nd: *People find it tempting to tell lies. Facts are not taken into consideration.* Be generous in your praise, if you think it's deserved. Lucky numbers: 5, 9.

Friday 3rd: *Quite an explosive time. Steady conditions could suddenly be upset.* A letter brings puzzling news. You'll be busy on the phone. Someone you need will be unavailable.

Saturday 4th: *Things don't flow easily. Expect mechanical troubles.* If you feel ill, medical treatment will be swift and sure. Have fun this evening, even if it costs.

Sunday 5th: *Edgy, restless day of arguments. Not a day to be shy or lonely.* Good day for dealing with youngsters. An evening out will be happy. Show your strength in a battle of wills.

Monday 6th: *A day of drawbacks, trouble or delays, silence or bad news.* You will enjoy some live entertainment. You may neglect chores, but who cares? Lucky colour: cream or white.

Tuesday 7th: *Some people will be scheming, going behind other people's backs.* Something nice will restore your faith in human nature. There's a chance of meeting someone special.

Wednesday 8th: *Travel plans run into difficulties. People are not easy-going.* You'll appreciate a lot of loving this evening! A long-time-no-see companion will be royally welcomed.

Thursday 9th: *You hear something intriguing. Still the promise of something unusual in the air.* People will support you if you get into trouble. You can't help feeling a bit of a fool.

Friday 10th: *People want something for nothing. A buzz of excitement in the air.* A romance at work should advance by leaps and bounds. Lucky numbers: 6, 9.

Saturday 11th: *Quite an explosive time. There could be a narrow escape.* At home a youngster has a madcap idea, and should be talked out of it. Don't be unfair to yourself.

Sunday 12th: *Lots of striving for success. An agreement could soon be reached.* You must keep a secret. People are relying on you. A contest goes well, and you'll feel successful.

Monday 13th: *A row breaks out between members of a group. Old heads are wiser than young hearts.* Good time to buy electronic goods. You are generous to others.

Tuesday 14th: *Reality catches up with those who have gone astray. Perhaps an escape comes to nothing.* You should wake up full of holiday fun. Aim to make other people happy.

Wednesday 15th: *People are slightly out of sorts with each other. An older person creates trouble.* If on holiday, you'll meet some cheerful company.

Thursday 16th: *Some aggro, but it sounds worse than it really is. Love tries to break out!* You are torn between two attitudes. In the end, you'll do what you're told.

Friday 17th: *Lots of optimism. The softer, kinder side of life wins for once.* A kiddie will need to be taught a lesson – but do it with humour. Good links with Aries and Leo.

Saturday 18th: *A really super day at last. You'll feel enthusiastic, hopeful and good-humoured.* Attend to a minor health complaint before it gets worse.

Sunday 19th: *An ideal family day. People should feel close and affectionate.* You want to be active. If forced to laze around, you'll get very frustrated.

Monday 20th: *An escapist day, perfect for getting away from daily routine.* Good week for selling something. You must reach a decision affecting others.

Tuesday 21st: *Striking day when there's an air of magic and excitement.* If entertaining at home, have plenty of food and drink. Happy links with Cancer and Scorpio.

Wednesday 22nd: *A sexy outlook on life. You'll be keen to see someone nice and attractive.* At work, there could be a mix-up over colleagues. Don't let them walk all over you.

Thursday 23rd: *High-powered time, with nothing going smoothly or steadily.* You may be kept waiting by professional people. If pulling up roots at this time, do it with confidence.

Friday 24th: *There could be a shift in family allegiances. Not an easy day.* Leave a fear at the back of your mind, where it can do no harm. Have a sexy evening, if possible.

Saturday 25th: *A time when reality catches up with you, perhaps in a special duty to perform.* A warm and loving evening, when a relationship will become more intimate.

Sunday 26th: *A day of shifting moods. You won't be able to keep track of people.* A relative isn't telling you the whole truth. It's better to be subtle than crass.

Monday 27th: *Something could be snatched away at the last moment.* The end of one phase of life and the start of a brand-new one. You seem excited and fearful at the same time.

Tuesday 28th: *Changeable day. People will be unreliable and impetuous.* There's a tendency to be extravagant without thinking. You're taking a partner too much for granted.

Wednesday 29th: *A graceful, artistic and intelligent day. You'll feel good and happy.* You may suffer from nerves for a while, after an emotional ordeal.

Thursday 30th: *Make the most of your social opportunities. Good day to make friends.* You must create excitement for yourself. If you think you're glamorous, others will agree!

Friday 31st: *Better luck. Good time to plan a fascinating venture.* A dog could do some damage when you're not looking. Small children are also a trial and a nuisance.

Wise Words for March

Democracy means government by discussion
but it is only effective
if you can stop people talking.

Clement Attlee

April
Guide

Something super could happen this April. There could be some lovely family news to celebrate, or in your personal life there could be a moment of triumph that pleases you, even if others aren't so happy.

Perhaps a decision you've been waiting for will finally emerge, or you'll be glad that you've made the right choice, after all.

One problem is that you've been worried about the behaviour of someone close to you. You may feel that they are changing – for the worse. By the same token, other people may find you a bit puzzling at the moment – not altogether sure of your motives, for instance.

WORK. There could indeed be big opportunities at work, but these must be balanced against your domestic duties.

You may be travelling more in the course of your work, or some Taureans could be moving overseas for a new contract.

Working conditions will be improved, and the link between you and a work-colleague, which has been bad in the past, now improves considerably.

If you work in the retail trade, there could be wonderful links with a special customer.

HOME. This is a reasonably settled month, with a sigh of relief that some relative is having a much better time.

There could be some extra expense associated with home, especially if you have visitors over the Easter break. If you are going abroad for a holiday, you may worry about the folks left at home – a little bit, anyway!

Older members of the family will side with you, even though they don't approve of everything you do.

A child – not necessarily your own – will bring joy one moment, anxiety the next.

HEALTH. It's a better time for Taurean men than women. It's a tricky time if you are expecting a child, as you may have to be more delicate with yourself than usual. There could also be increased period cramps, menopausal difficulties and the like.

There could also be problems with feet, especially with in-growing toenails, corns and even a broken bone through a careless fall.

MONEY. It seems a generous-hearted month when you will be extravagant with the cash available. But you will still like value for money, and won't appreciate being over-charged.

Children's spending money needs careful control, too. If you have a youngster shooting up, he or she will need new clothes every few months this year.

If you are a gambler, the new Flat season could bring you some early winners, and if you try a new system that's strongly touted in the papers you'll find it works well – to start with.

LEISURE. Someone may stop you from having your own brand of fun, and you won't take kindly to this interference.

There could be a slight clash of interests with a good friend, meaning you won't see so much of each other, over the next few months. If you're a keen sports person, you could be girding yourself up for the new season ahead. It's also a good social time, especially for travel, the theatre, music and the concert hall.

Watch out for something pleasureable to do with antiques, plus the chance to dress up – in fancy dress?

LOVE. This could be a very lively month for you. A stale old relationship, be it a marriage or old love affair could suddenly revive, while a brand-new romance could begin on a terrific note of enthusiasm and sexiness.

In the second half of April in particular, you seem in a passionate mood, and won't want to take no for an answer. If courting, you should make a big effort now – and if you don't succeed, you try, try again!

You seem to get on particularly well with Gemini and Leo folk, though less happily with other Taureans in your life.

April
Key Dates

Saturday 1st: *Wonderful family time, with marvellous links with someone you love.* There's a scarcity of something you want. Lucky numbers: 3, 8.

Sunday 2nd: *Still an enjoyable time, with a zip in the air. Very loving and friendly.* If you share your home with others, there could soon be a new arrival.

Monday 3rd: *Everything goes well. A friendly, sociable time. Romance is really favoured.* In business a person in authority can prove a real help.

Tuesday 4th: *Cheerful and happy. Things go with a swing, though you mustn't be silly.* Try and get a moment to yourself, to plan where you're going.

Wednesday 5th: *Still lively and forward-looking. The man in the house causes upsets.* There could be news of an inheritance now or in the future.

Thursday 6th: *Muddles get sorted out. People are more peaceful though there's still an explosive air.* Good time to give up something – you'll find it easier than you fear.

Friday 7th: *Marginally up-tight and bottled up. A nice chance for relaxation, too.* You can be lucky with a horse beginning with A or F. Go out for an evening meal.

Saturday 8th: *There are worries about personal relationships. The truth comes tumbling out.* You are quite psychic at the moment, and will pick up strange feelings.

Sunday 9th: *Deals are struck. A day of good fortune and new possibilities.* You can bring happiness where it isn't expected. Show affection, and you'll be loved in return.

Monday 10th: *Happy day for most, but a nasty shock comes to some.* There will be annoying changes in your neighbourhood. A face you'd sooner forget may turn up again.

Tuesday 11th: *Easy-going day. Not many demands being placed on people.* Gadgets that haven't been used recently will be broken or run down. This could be a day of decision.

Wednesday 12th: *An excellent time to feel that you belong to a* *group. A great sense of family and togetherness.* A cash arrangement is soon coming to an end.

Thursday 13th: *A sexy and flamboyant day for many. Sudden passion erupts!* Make financial decisions with confidence; things look brighter for most of 1989.

Friday 14th: *Little arguments and minor altercations, but no big problems.* Things won't be the same again for some Taurus folk, after an interesting weekend ahead.

Saturday 15th: *Sweetness gets the better of anger. A kiss-and-make-up time.* Things will work out better than expected. You're in a naughty but nice mood!

Sunday 16th: *Slightly at sixes and sevens. A friendly row may turn into an open quarrel.* If you're feeling low, you'll soon be better. Love finds a way, even in difficulties.

Monday 17th: *A way is found out of one difficulty. A dogged day, but you get through.* You could be forgotten in a plan of action by others. Someone puts undue pressure on you.

Tuesday 18th: *A lively, restless time with many small changes in the offing.* At work you will enjoy yourself. You're lucky with favourites this afternoon.

Wednesday 19th: *Energetic time. Real feelings will burst out. A surprise for many folk.* Give the go-ahead to a child who wants to do something different.

Thursday 20th: *A sensible day, but there's plenty of imagination and sensitivity, too.* A stranger will help you, but don't get too friendly or someone will get the wrong idea.

Friday 21st: *A sober day time, with a lot of catching up to do. Neglected tasks have mounted up.* A big shopping trip will be a success. A child could have a fall.

Saturday 22nd: *A happy day. Some unpleasantness will be forgiven or forgotten.* A girl friend will egg you on. No time to be shy – be bold and you'll get what you want.

Sunday 23rd: *A warm-hearted weekend, ideal for socializing and romance.* Someone will keep you guessing. I think you're too shy to make a fuss. Suddenly things go badly.

Monday 24th: *A day of sunlight and shadows. Some good news, but problems as well.* A sweetheart could spring a lovely surprise on you. Worries can be put to the back of your mind.

Tuesday 25th: *Hard-thinking time. A bright idea meets an* *obstinate obstacle.* Your partner is in more of a home-loving mood, while you want to go and paint the town red.

Wednesday 26th: *Something old and outworn will hold you back. A better time for romance.* You're able to twist someone round your little finger. Great links with someone foreign.

Thursday 27th: *A more sensible mood arrives. People with experience take charge.* You may act as go-between. A neighbour has some bad news, and will be affected.

Friday 28th: *The start of a nice weekend for family togetherness. Terrific for artistic activity.* If out of work, try to maintain interest in a hobby that could one day earn money.

Saturday 29th: *You feel lucky, but it may all be a chimera. Don't count your chickens.* An affectionate day. You'll get what you want from people around you – by being kind.

Sunday 30th: *You'll be glad to put the bad times behind you. A luckier mood altogether.* A friend will be rather snobbish, which is a shame. A great day to go somewhere fresh.

Wise Words for April

Some people will believe anything –
if you whisper it to them.
Louis B. Nizer

May
Guide

If big events happened in March or April, you will spend May settling down, feeling your way into a new job, a fresh relationship or a different home. Even if none of these things happen, you'll be jogging along, happily enough, but your scene may not be as exciting as you would like.

For some Taureans your thoughts will be far away, wondering what someone else is doing, and perhaps planning how you can see them again soon.

You are going to be pleasant company, sociable and good-humoured, but you may feel that you are into a routine stretch and getting nowhere.

WORK. One effort may be wasted, and have to be repeated. You may work hard for little money, and feel your efforts aren't appreciated enough.

You're happy with your work-colleagues, though you could be missing a gang of people you used to work with.

If you are still in your same job, a new arrival will find it hard to settle down, and you will have to make an effort to make them feel at home.

HOME. You're in an amiable critical mood, inclined to nag relatives because they aren't keeping up to scratch.

If you don't hear from one relative who's away, you'll be inclined to worry, even though there's no cause for alarm. Otherwise it's a good time for a family get-together, but there may be a farewell involved, too.

If you share rooms with other people besides your family, there could be a growing sense of tension, perhaps over one item that gets lost, or behaviour that you find unsocial.

There could be drama concerning relatives who live elsewhere, especially grown-up brothers or sisters.

HEALTH. It's important that you don't over-exert yourself, especially if you've had a fairly sedentary job for a long while.

At the same time, irregular meals or too much junk food could quickly lead to kidney or liver trouble.

If there has been an accident recently, a wound looks slow to heal, and a bone slow to knit together. Your doctor may not seem anxious, but it will seem an irritant to you.

MONEY. Once again, luck seems to be on your side. You could get a bonus, a tax repayment or some other one-off sum.

It's a good time to get into gilts, which will enjoy a run of luck in the next two months. Both silver and gold will drop in price, but there could be a large take-over involving an electrical or engineering company.

You'll be spending more than usual on garden furniture, plants, patio equipment and the like. It's a good time to be changing your bank, getting a new source of finance, or perhaps joining a new building society.

If you enjoy gambling, your lucky weeks are the first and third. You have a terrific run of luck from the 17th onward.

LEISURE. There could be a special entertainment or outing linked with your place of work, and you'll all have a terrific time on that.

Music, singing or dancing will be an enjoyable kind of entertainment this month, and you may make a special trip to another town in order to have a rave or see a rare entertainment.

You'll be spending weekends away from home more than usual, especially if there's a new friend living in the country.

LOVE. It looks a wonderfully romantic month from the second week onwards. Someone may return into your life, bringing a great glow of happiness, and a relationship which seemed tame and boring up till now will suddenly become sexy and possessive. There's every chance of emotional happiness, when your libido should be riding high. Taureans by the end of the month should be full of sex appeal.

You get on particularly well with Scorpio and Capricorn folk, less so with Gemini or Virgo.

May
Key Dates

Monday 1st: *A day of low spirits. Someone could do the dirty on you.* Beware of a small accident caused through silly carelessness.

Tuesday 2nd: *A day to speak your mind. You have lots of persuasive power.* There could be a nice friendship developing through your work. Lucky numbers: 5, 7.

Wednesday 3rd: *Pleasant day, with people lucky out of the blue, and good news arriving.* Today seems lucky, though you may not receive as much as you'd like.

Thursday 4th: *A real sense of achievement for many people. Good for travel.* In sport you may fail through the mistakes of others. The evening makes up for everything.

Friday 5th: *Basically cheerful, but something unusual, even weird, could happen.* There should be a better atmosphere between man and wife. There are fights between children, though.

Saturday 6th: *Legal problems will finally start to be solved. There's luck in a serious matter.* You will have a lucky break, especially in the company of a friend.

Sunday 7th: *Quite a lucky day. People want to make a fresh beginning.* Better weather should be making you happy. Excellent time to be out in the fresh air.

Monday 8th: *People are prepared to take the risk. A day when the public is heard.* There could be support from an unexpected quarter. Financially you could make a surprise gain.

Tuesday 9th: *A chopping and changing day. People are getting used to new conditions.* There could be changes at work that leave you puzzled. Keep your nose to the grindstone.

Wednesday 10th: *Versatile day. People will try something new, and like it.* Colour schemes are buzzing through your head, but you won't finalize redecorating plans for a while.

Thursday 11th: *A tougher, hard-nosed time, with a strong whiff of success – for some.* You may make a decision on your summer holiday – and it will be a slightly unusual choice.

Friday 12th: *Quite cheerful in the circumstances. Basically a loving, supportive day.* There could be trouble over travel, also an injury if playing sport.

Saturday 13th: *Very lucky day for some people. A blessing comes out of the blue.* Romance is favoured. Get away together, and you'll have a terrific time without the others.

Sunday 14th: *Still a lively time in love. People look for something spicy.* You need something jolly and colourful in your life. Don't doubt and criticize so much.

Monday 15th: *Amiable day. Things get forgotten or pushed to one side.* Get onto a repair job fast. Encourage a friend to try something new. Lucky colours for you: grey and green.

Tuesday 16th: *Pleasant, warm-hearted day. People seem perky and friendly.* Plenty of energy and high spirits. If you're feeling low, you'll soon be better.

Wednesday 17th: *More serious. People will work hard for a long time.* There could be a contest between your partner and you. Expect a fight at work over what's to be done.

Thursday 18th: *People will find it hard to think straight, but they are sexy and escapist.* There's some bad temper today, or a clash of personalities. Be strong-minded but fair.

Friday 19th: *Travel problems if you're on the roads. There could be a lucky break, though.* If out of work, you can find a voluntary job that's a lot of fun. You need a push.

Saturday 20th: *Still an uncertain time, great if you have no responsibilities.* This weekend involves you in a lot of activities. You'll be tired out by bedtime.

Sunday 21st: *Temper, temper! Everyone seems touchy today. Not an easy time.* You mix with another family, and enjoy yourself. Travel is definitely favoured.

Monday 22nd: *A lucky day for many folk. Guesses and hunches are likely to be right.* You feel generous, but your gift may not be appreciated. Never mind, try something else.

Tuesday 23rd: *An oddball day. People will appear arrogant and conceited.* There could be happy family news centring on a young child. There are favourable links with abroad.

Wednesday 24th: *Amid a broadly happy day there could be one slap in the face.* A family problem seems easier. Someone who hasn't been able to cope will be more confident now.

Thursday 25th: *People want to explain their feelings. A persuasive day.* If you meet a beautiful (or handsome) stranger, you'll make a good impression – but will it go anywhere?

Friday 26th: *Some anger and short temper, but it will soon blow over.* You'll be sorry you threw something away. There's a use for it now. Lucky numbers: 1, 8.

Saturday 27th: *Friendly within the family. Still a practical time, and a tiring one.* Expect quarrels at home. You'll be glad to get out and about with your mates.

Sunday 28th: *Still a potentially violent time. Don't expect a quiet time.* You hear some juicy gossip. If entertaining at the weekend, do things in style.

Monday 29th: *A muddle will lead to a firm decision. Quite good for the family.* Quite a passionate week, and Taureans will feel a great need to be romantic.

Tuesday 30th: *A more relaxed time. You have an appetite for something new and different.* You may be moody and vulnerable at this stage of the working week.

Wednesday 31st: *Quite hard-working, but it's not easy to concentrate on the job in hand.* Friendship with a younger person will prosper. You want to be daring, but may be held back.

Wise Words for May

A good holiday is one spent among people
whose notions of time are vaguer than yours.

J.B. Priestley

June
Guide

The first half of June is a doubtful time, when you may be uncertain about someone else's plans or be unsure what you yourself are going to do. You may be having second thoughts, or someone may be trying to persuade you round to their way of thinking. Probably you'll change your mind.

Certainly it doesn't seem a very active time – indeed, you could be pleasantly lazy and putting something off because you can't be bothered. Life's too short for that.

Other people treat you well this month. You seem in a winning mood, though not through any great exertion on your part. You'll be good company – not sparkling so much as comfortable to be with. You do want to be popular.

WORK. The firm or organization you work for could be involved in delicate negotiations at present, so everything's up in the air. It's not the time to rock the boat – stay discreet and respect any confidences you may hear.

You'll find it easy to work with the people around you, including a boss who has been disagreeable in his time. If you are a creative worker, you're in a fine inventive frame of mind this June, and will be full of bright ideas. In particular, if you work in advertising, public relations, sales or design, you'll have a terrific time. There could be promotion beckoning.

HOME. It's a fairly affable, relaxed time, though there may be a few friendly arguments within the home. If one member of the family is taking exams this year, it won't be quite as tense and tricky an atmosphere as you'd feared.

You may be saddened by the departure of one or two neighbours, especially if one leaves in a hurry. If a local place is up for sale, you may be fearful about the arrivals – but everything works out well in the end.

HEALTH. Part of your winning streak involves your good health, and you should be feeling fit as a fiddle around now.

You aren't in an effortful frame of mind, so I doubt if you'll be taking much exercise or losing much weight, but at least you shouldn't feel poorly.

If you have got a chronic illness, you may find that spiritual healing somehow works wonders around now. There could be some kind of charismatic meeting in your neighbourhood, to which you're strongly drawn.

MONEY. You seem full of plans for the month ahead, but this will mean a big outlay of funds. You must get your priorities right, or there'll be nothing left for food.

If you're taking a holiday this month, incidental expenses will be much higher than expected, but you'll have to shrug and bear the pain. It'll all be worthwhile.

Investments should show steady growth at this time, and you'll be pleased that a shrewd guess earlier in the year has been proved right by now.

LEISURE. There may be a new entertainment or sports centre coming to your district, and you'll find the money – and enthusiasm – to play a big part in it.

It's a good time to attend a festival or visit a special exhibition. If you're playing sport, you won't feel like doing much training, but will rely on verve and flair on the day itself.

LOVE. Although you're sexy quite a bit of the time, it may not coincide with the moment when your partner is.

Your nicest times are the first and fourth weeks. The second week looks a bit tricky, when you could have a momentary break-up. But all ends well.

If you are lonesome and looking for a friend, this is an excellent month for finding a new sweetheart. It could be in unexpected circumstances, and perhaps an unexpected person. If you've always felt you liked the boy next door, it could be someone foreign and exotic that you set your heart on.

You are particularly drawn to Aquarian and Sagittarian types at present, but not so much to Cancer and Virgo.

June
Key Dates

Thursday 1st: *You want to break free from a boring, up-tight situation.* Today is best spent quietly on your own. Too many people will bore you.

Friday 2nd: *The tail-end of a difficult working week. Not a time to feel brilliantly happy.* You should whizz through your daily chores. There's a disappointment in your leisure hours.

Saturday 3rd: *Some black moods, obstinacy and deliberate bloody-mindedness.* On holiday you'll make interesting friends, perhaps foreigners. You'll be moved by an artistic experience.

Sunday 4th: *A smooth routine gets upset. Good links with the family.* You are in a warm-hearted mood this evening, full of affection. You'll show off in front of others.

Monday 5th: *Slight delay is possible, but otherwise a lucky time – in love and money.* You can have a say in the future – but you won't get your own way entirely.

Tuesday 6th: *A good day for working hard until the job is finished.* There is a new scheme that can protect savings against inflation. Don't be scared of an official.

Wednesday 7th: *Still a great influence, as far as the family is concerned.* An older relative will grumble a good deal. You'll be glad to get away from an oppressive atmosphere.

Thursday 8th: *A day of serious thinking, with a hope soon to be realized.* Don't be pushed around by an official. Enjoy life with younger people. Music will greatly move you.

Friday 9th: *Still a warm, pleasant and loving time bringing people together.* Your taste is changing. What you loved once will seem boring now. Lucky colours: red, grey.

Saturday 10th: *Pleasant weekend, but you need to tackle something energetic.* You may worry unduly about someone who is perfectly all right. Relax and enjoy yourself.

Sunday 11th: *Wonderful weekend for falling in love. Success for many people.* Get your facts right – or you could make a fool of yourself. Look for someone with the initial A or H.

Monday 12th: *A wonderful day. Make the most of any opportunity coming your way.* You can help to keep something open, or a local service running. Lucky numbers: 5, 10.

Tuesday 13th: *Muddled time. Lies will be told. But warm-hearted too, so perhaps a reconciliation.* Pay a lot of attention to the opposite sex, as you've bags of subtle sexual charisma.

Wednesday 14th: *Unsettled day. Perhaps there's a promise of more difficulties to come.* Lay off the booze if you're starting to feel bad. Give as good as you get.

Thursday 15th: *Low spirits for a while. There could be a delay or disappointment.* There could be a small breakage at home. At work there's a row breaking out.

Friday 16th: *A day of surprises and shocks. People are looking for something different.* A mechanism could let you down. You won't be able to repair it on your own.

Saturday 17th: *Pleasantly energetic time. A bright idea could solve everything.* Now is the time to make an important change in your outlook. Not a lazy weekend.

Sunday 18th: *Still lucky. Ideal time to feel love for someone close to you.* There's good co-operation within the family circle. Friends and family will mix well.

Monday 19th: *Quite a relaxed, happy-go-lucky time, but with an underlying melancholy.* You are feeling stand-offish in a romance, and won't want to be taken for granted.

Tuesday 20th: *Some people will be stubborn and old-fashioned. Bloody-minded day.* You seem in an artistic mood, especially for making or choosing clothes.

Wednesday 21st: *Doubts abound, but you'll still trust to luck. An untrustworthy day.* Make phone calls early, as problems will arise – and you need time to sort them out.

Thursday 22nd: *Lots of optimism, keeping fingers crossed, and hoping for the best.* Support someone at work who is receiving rough justice. Spend the evening in pleasant company.

Friday 23rd: *Not the day to step out of line, especially in romance.* A horse that did badly last time out can romp home for you today. This evening you need comfort and cuddles.

Saturday 24th: *Sweet-natured time when toughness gives way to sentimentality.* Don't allow anyone owing you money to get away with it. There could be ear, nose or throat trouble.

Sunday 25th: *Still the possibility of disruption. People do not seem to want peaceful solutions.* You must be serious about a child's problems. Don't allow a spoilt brat to spoil things.

Monday 26th: *People want to take risks – without working out the risks involved!* Definitely the week when you should take charge if other people seem inadequate.

Tuesday 27th: *There's a feeling that something's gotta give! Slightly muddled time.* A solid sort of day when other people may find you rather square and conventional.

Wednesday 28th: *Rows within the family, but it's better out than bottled up.* You are worried about your standard of living, and must give something up.

Thursday 29th: *You'll hear the sharp edge of someone's tongue. An excitable day.* It's a good time to commit yourself to a course of action this summer.

Friday 30th: *A day of deception and muddle. Someone could be deceiving you.* A quiet day – by evening you'll be looking for fun. If you're the flighty sort, you start a new romance.

Wise Words for June

He knows not his own strength
that hath not met adversity.
Ben Jonson

July
Guide

You should be in a happy mood this month. You're feeling amiable and affectionate and out-going, and you're not as selfish and self-centred as you can sometimes be.

It seems as though you are promoting someone else's interests – their talent, their hopes, their attractiveness – but whatever the reason you are being very persuasive and will swing people round to your way of thinking.

In your own personal life there should be a feeling of buoyancy. A close relationship may be getting much better or a new one suddenly develops. Or, if you have been emotionally trapped for years, this could be the time when you break free.

WORK. You should have a really good time at work this month. You may be getting together with work-mates to enjoy yourselves in off-duty hours, or you may develop one particular new friend at work. This could mark a brief office romance.

There could be one moment of disappointment early in July, and, if you run your own business, you could find that a promised area of co-operation suddenly turns nasty.

If you have just started a new job, you make a good impression. If you are expecting exam results this month, they should be more favourable than expected, and nudge you in a new direction.

HOME. There could be a spot of family quarrelling this month. You yourself may be feeling restless, wanting to pull up roots and move elsewhere, or there could be a clash with older members of the family. If you are young yourself, you want to do your own thing, but they want you to stay a child.

The fabric of the house may need some attention, but if the damage has been caused by someone else – or an act of God – you may have difficulty in getting recompense.

If you are wanting to move, there could be anxiety that a deal will not go through. Have faith!

HEALTH. Your cheerful mood should mean a cheerful and healthy demeanour. There's nothing much wrong with you at this time.

If you were having problems with a pregnancy, things should now have sorted themselves out. There's a slight danger of a skin infection, but it won't linger.

There could be a little eye disease, especially if you have been swimming in an unfamiliar swimming pool. Beware of pink-eye, conjunctivitis, etc.

MONEY. It is not quite such a lucky time as that you have enjoyed in the last couple of months, but there is still a feeling that money could turn up out of nowhere.

It's a good month for selling things that you have grown or made yourself, be they vegetables, flowers, arts or crafts. But beware of anyone calling wanting to buy some other possession. It might be more valuable than you realize.

If you want to gamble, you'll find yourself doing well at horse-racing in the second and third weeks.

LEISURE. It continues to be an entertaining month, and you'll enjoy group activities whether with work-mates, friends or family.

You aren't in the mood to do heavy labouring yourself around the garden or anywhere, neither will you really enjoy a self-catering holiday. For once you really want to be pampered.

If an unexpected party invitation comes, make the most of it. You could have a couple of weekends away from home, one with well-to-do friends whom you get to know much better.

Watch out for a visiting cultural entertainment.

LOVE. Basically a loving and happy month, though there may be a conscience pricking you in the background. Some Taureans will be having an extra-marital love affair, which, while very nice in itself, could be causing ructions in your heart.

A fairly new romance should be turning nicely into a settling-down phase. But in-laws or old friends of your sweetheart may prove a bit interfering at times.

You get on well with Sagittarius and Pisces at present, not quite so happily with Gemini or Virgo.

July
Key Dates

Saturday 1st: *Wonderful links with other folk. People want to co-operate.* There may be a clash with an elderly person, so be courteous.

Sunday 2nd: *A steady, comfortable day when the elderly are honoured.* You will think fondly of the past – in romance especially. You're the life and soul of the party.

Monday 3rd: *Bags of energy and enjoyment. You should have a stroke of good fortune.* There could be a clash of principles with someone. Lucky colours: gold, blue.

Tuesday 4th: *A give-and-take day. There'll be tough talking, but agreement finally.* You may have to deal with a strong-minded individual, but you'll get your own way.

Wednesday 5th: *Still a pleasant, hard-working time with folk getting on well.* Don't take 'no' for an answer. Try another tack, or go somewhere new for fresh advice.

Thursday 6th: *Head and heart go different ways. Not an unhappy time.* Your social scene should be brightening up. A new acquaintance is great fun, once you know him or her.

Friday 7th: *People are not inclined to give way. Hard-talking, fast-acting day.* If you've been ill, there could be a sudden recovery. You gain from an older person.

Saturday 8th: *Lively and unconventional, but within sensible limits.* Other people's spending habits will be on your mind, but there's no easy way to put things right.

Sunday 9th: *Worry about an underlying state of affairs. This is a sobering day.* You could even break the law, without realizing it. Keep away from mischief.

Monday 10th: *People can talk themselves into – or out of – love. A sociable, conversational day.* A phone call will clear up some nagging doubts. You may need professional help.

Tuesday 11th: *Lovely family mood. Sensible plans will be made for the future.* There will be some unexpected company – and not altogether welcome.

Wednesday 12th: *Arguments and discord. There's a hue and cry*

66

over something important. An old friend needs cheering up, which you can do. A place that's been a favourite may close.

Thursday 13th: *Ideal get-away-from-it-all day, great for travel by air.* Your partner is looking for a cuddly evening, but you aren't in the mood.

Friday 14th: *More energetic, but still an escapist, anti-realistic time.* You must teach someone good manners. It does no harm to be strong-minded about this.

Saturday 15th: *If there's an obstacle, break it down! Not a day for half-measures!* Aim for a relaxing weekend – tiredness will lead to illness. You'll grumble about service, if out.

Sunday 16th: *A sexy weekend. Older people are appreciated. But one group of people are stubborn.* A cheerful day when your personality is at its brightest.

Monday 17th: *Quite restless. A new idea could solve an old problem.* You have difficulty in collecting money from people. A delay proves a blessing in disguise.

Tuesday 18th: *Good working day. Plenty can be achieved. Youth and age co-operate nicely.* A phone call out of the blue will set your mind buzzing with ideas.

Wednesday 19th: *Plans could start to fall apart. You're unsure where you stand.* It's a specially good time for Taurus women – in career, in politics, in love.

Thursday 20th: *Good atmosphere at work. A time to get rid of a state of affairs that's outworn.* Love is in the air, but your lover is waiting for you to show your real feelings.

Friday 21st: *Still a sexy time. Lots of desire and appeal for people.* If you meet new people you'll find plenty in common. You'll be moved by the beauty of nature – and romance.

Saturday 22nd: *Much better. There will be a good rapport and communication between people.* An unlikely betting tip is crazy – but tempting! There's lots happening this evening.

Sunday 23rd: *A day when people with experience should be heard. Quite a lucky time.* Keep a special eye on careless drivers, especially after dark. One of your preoccupied days.

Monday 24th: *Some difficulties, but you have the ingenuity to overcome them.* Things look better on the health front – if you've been in pain, it should lessen.

Tuesday 25th: *A super day, making up for the troubles of the* *last day or two.* Your partner is in more of a home-loving mood, while you want to go and paint the town red.

Wednesday 26th: *Thrifty time, so watch your pennies. Still a warm-hearted phase.* Your partner is full of summer joy, and will try to cheer you up.

Thursday 27th: *You can't do exactly what you want. Rather a rebellious day.* There's a mystery in your life. Perhaps something disappears, or someone is keeping news from you.

Friday 28th: *Energetic end to the working week. Quite a lot will be achieved.* At work you can earn good marks. The evening is a time to get right away.

Saturday 29th: *Nice weekend, but one member of the family could be fractious.* You'll be roused from laziness by a surprise event. You're very competitive, and want to play sport.

Sunday 30th: *Something finally gets finished. The end of an era? A new beginning?* Put on a charming face, even if you're not up to it. A young friend gives happiness.

Monday 31st: *Fairly pleasant, up-beat day, with some good news. Stay merry and bright.* You will be found very attractive by someone you work with.

Wise Words for July

We are all in the gutter,
but some of us are looking at the stars.
Oscar Wilde

August
Guide

You could be caught up in one or two practical tasks early in August that demand your full attention. If you are having building work done around the house, it will prove more expensive and time-consuming than you expected.

If you hear exam results this month, you have a good chance of doing well, but a job that you thought was promised may turn out to be less than reliable. Never mind, there's going to be another chance soon.

You could also be busy poking your nose into someone else's business – perhaps a brother or sister's – without realizing that you're causing offence. This sounds prying, but probably you can be genuinely helpful.

WORK. If there has been a background worry in the last few weeks, it should get sorted out in the second week of August.

During this first half of the month you'll take great pride in your work. It's an especially good time if you are a skilled craftsperson, but it's also good for getting promotion to a new kind of work or for moving to a new job that will call for new skills.

Even if you keep your present job, you could be working in different surroundings for a while, or taking the place of someone else who's away.

HOME. Quarrels could continue at home, particularly between the generations. They're not really serious, but it means that you're not entirely happy with the people you're living with.

If you share a flat with friends, you could well be on the move yourself, or perhaps homeless for a couple of months while you take a holiday abroad. There seems to be a flux in your affairs which is not really worrying – indeed, quite pleasurable – though you won't be certain quite where you end up. Some young Taureans, for instance, could be moving in with a sweetheart, and you're doubtful what the family response will be.

HEALTH. You remain pretty fit. Even if you have a chronic complaint its symptoms will be much less than usual. If you are disabled, there could be some new device on the market that enables you to get around more easily.

If you have been mentally disturbed for some time, there could be a sudden reason why your mind and spirits are much happier from now on. In particular, if you have suffered from a phobia in the past, some event this month could suddenly free you from your fears.

MONEY. Beware of accepting a job where the money isn't quite right. If you don't get the right economic security, you'll worry about it for ages.

If travelling abroad, there is always the danger of theft, so take travellers' cheques rather than just straight cash.

If you want to be lucky, your gambling luck comes back in the third week, and you could have beginner's luck if you go to a casino, for instance.

LEISURE. It is definitely the month for holidays, and all kinds of hobbies, sports and amusements will please you. There may be a clash with a family duty towards the end of the month, but you'll still try and get your own way.

You will certainly be going to more parties than usual, though you may get fed up with the constant round of social fun. You need a bit of time to yourself.

LOVE. You seem quite happy about life, and even if there are worries about your love life you will still be enjoying the exciting bits! Your sexual libido is powerful this month.

You may feel it is time to consider your long-term future, but your partner will not be so co-operative about this.

A new romance may turn out to be someone from a very different background to your own. This will be quite exciting at first, but it doesn't promise well for a long-term relationship.

As for partners, your best Zodiac links this month are Pisces and Gemini. They're such fun.

August
Key Dates

Tuesday 1st: *Time to count the cost – but you're still in an extravagant mood.* Good time to plan ahead, fixing up dates in the future.

Wednesday 2nd: *People won't want to be cooped up. A lively, adventurous day.* Good time for handling money. People keep you waiting. There's an air of adventure in your life.

Thursday 3rd: *An angry day. People may lash out on the least pretext.* You could be forgotten in a plan of action by others. Don't get bored with your own company.

Friday 4th: *Start of a fast-moving weekend, edgy and restless. But a good-humoured time.* You can't concentrate on work, so a mistake will be made in the afternoon.

Saturday 5th: *Still a frank, no-holds-barred day. Good time to start new groups.* Romance looks happiest this afternoon, if you should be so lucky!

Sunday 6th: *Well-meaning day. Some delays, but not serious ones.* The end of one phase of life and the start of a brand-new one. Maybe you'll be saying goodbye to someone.

Monday 7th: *The imagination gets wild and woolly. Good for creative work.* You have some extra charisma today. You'll really shine among friends, also among work-mates.

Tuesday 8th: *More changeable still – and still something happens to leave no further doubts.* Stay wrapped up against cold winds, especially near the sea. Good for entering a contest.

Wednesday 9th: *Success could be in sight, after a long, hard struggle.* You cannot wait any longer for someone who's always slow. Have fun, play a practical joke.

Thursday 10th: *Cheerful day when people exaggerate. Good for a party.* At work it pays to be forthright; you may have to stand up to your boss.

Friday 11th: *A sudden surprise in love. Good time to catch a stranger's eye.* Things brighten today, and by the weekend you're full of the joys of spring.

Saturday 12th: *Slightly accident-prone day, but still a sexy time.* If you meet someone important or well-to-do, you'll get tongue-tied. Try to admit faults fast among friends.

Sunday 13th: *Slight aggro over nothing. People are looking for arguments.* With your own sweetheart you can have a good time in the evening with another couple. A foursome is great.

Monday 14th: *The bad mood lifts. This looks more sprightly and interesting.* You've got a lot going for you. It looks an extravagant time, but a generous-hearted one, too.

Tuesday 15th: *Really quite a wonderful day, with lots of sweetness and grace.* No one will give you any aggro today. Everything looks great, especially if you're on holiday.

Wednesday 16th: *A terrific day, with nothing hindering folk from having a good time.* You can bring romance back into your life, with a kindly thought.

Thursday 17th: *Hot-blooded time, with a good chance of success. Go for it!* You wake with a bright new idea. Do something positive with your lunch hour.

Friday 18th: *An extravagant time. If in doubt, spend! A great time to make new friends.* A good idea must be shelved for the time being. But the evening looks great.

Saturday 19th: *More cheerful. Luck's in the air. There's a silver lining to that cloud!* Have a clean-out of a room, cupboard, kitchen or car. You could make an unexpected discovery.

Sunday 20th: *Minor criticisms spoil the overall mood. Folk are out of sorts with each other.* Your future looks slightly muddled. You are faced by several choices.

Monday 21st: *Good for talks, negotiations, deals – but some folk are out to make trouble.* You'll have a good time, and appear confident, even if you're nervous underneath.

Tuesday 22nd: *Quite lucky and extravagant and flirty – great for having fun.* Today could bring you a couple of winners. You'll enjoy a good book or a great story-teller.

Wednesday 23rd: *Time to count cash and be thrifty. A stylish day, and a glamorous one.* If you have a bad-tempered spouse, you'll soon laugh him (or her) out of a black mood.

Thursday 24th: *A sprightly day, with one or two surprises. It's a loving time for most.* You may have to deal with someone with a disability – if so, do it with a glad heart.

Friday 25th: *Slight quarrels at home. Mothers seem to get the worst of it.* There's more to life than money. Definitely the time to enjoy the simple things in life.

Saturday 26th: *Good weekend for travel and adventure, ideal for sport.* Be lucky with an outsider. Don't let the moaners get you down. You need plenty of exercise.

Sunday 27th: *Very loving time, ideal for reconciliation or first love.* You must look after yourself, as promised help may not arrive. Someone with the initial C or K is helpful.

Monday 28th: *Nice steady day. You need to have a purpose in life to enjoy yourself.* Check on a neighbour, though, who may be lonely. Count your pennies – some may be missing.

Tuesday 29th: *Success could suddenly crown a complicated issue.* A friend could be in trouble, and you can give the right help. Have a serious talk about the future.

Wednesday 30th: *You can't stay in a rut. Smooth running will be disrupted.* A love affair will prosper – indeed, you should be delighted with the attention you receive.

Thursday 31st: *A careful, painstaking day – but there may still be a surprise.* Make an effort to be pleasant, even though you don't feel like it.

Wise Words for August

Misfortunes when asleep
are not to be awakened.
English proverb

September
Guide

This seems a month of change. At the start of September you're quite set in your ways, and reasonably happy, but towards the end of the month you'll realize that a big decision has to be made, and this could get you restless and edgy. There could be several friendly arguments, but not the final clash that you expect.

People will continue to find you interesting company, and you should remain popular. But one person's hostility will be directed almost personally towards you, and you can't understand the reason why.

It is a month that calls for courage and risk. You must be prepared to jump out of your Taurean caution into a more fluid situation.

WORK. For some Taureans there will be a big career-change around now, something which has been foreshadowed in the last few months. If you do make a change, it will be for the better. There's no need to be fearful about leaving a relatively pleasant place of work.

If you have been jobless for some time, you stand an excellent chance of getting an exciting job around now – perhaps at the last minute, perhaps because someone else dropped out. Never mind, it's yours now.

HOME. Some Taureans will be having domestic changes around this time. Children could be leaving home to go to college or set up home elsewhere, or you yourself could be settling into a new residence – perhaps with someone new.

There isn't much time for spare-time activities if you have to concentrate on smartening the place up, making it feel more like your home. If you are doing the place up, it will cost more than you expect, and you may have to ration out the improvements over the next few months.

HEALTH. It is certainly a beneficial and healing time when spiritual healing could work very well for you. But beware in mid-September of a careless moment that could cause an electric shock.

You certainly care a lot about your looks, and will be making strenuous efforts to improve them. If you are thinking about cosmetic surgery for instance, this is an excellent time to have it done.

In much the same way, a new beauty treatment or completely fresh hairstyle will do you the world of good.

MONEY. It's not an easy time if you have to handle other people's finances for them. You could find it a tremendous muddle, especially if money-matters have been neglected in the past.

There could be some extra cash for you, however, due to an improved salary or part-time work in the evenings.

If you're an investor, you will do well in shares with a hotel group or stores group. The entertainment and leisure sector should improve considerably in the next six months – so be part of the bandwagon yourself.

LEISURE. If there's something special organized this month, it may take a lot of work getting ready for it, and then not be quite so much fun when it arrives.

You don't seem to have too much leisure time at present. If you have moved somewhere new, you may be half-missing your friends – and half-pleased that you don't have to see them so much!

Although you remain popular, you may be making an effort to move to a new social circle – with conspicuous success, though it all takes time.

LOVE. It is a very passionate and sexy start to the month, but then you pass through an interim phase during the second and third weeks when you aren't so interested in love-making.

If you're young and fancy-free, you'll be radiating lots of charm and sexiness by the end of September. This is an excellent time to reunite with someone who pleased you greatly earlier in the year – but then drifted away.

September
Key Dates

Friday 1st: *Nice start to the month. You feel warm and sexy! Good relations with others.* You should be getting on top of a difficult situation.

Saturday 2nd: *A kindly and well-intentioned time. No one is trying to trick anyone.* Visitors at home will bring a surprise present. If you go out, it will be expensive.

Sunday 3rd: *A sober day thinking about the future. Something new will crop up.* You wake with a bright new idea. But others pour cold water on your plans.

Monday 4th: *The same mixture – sunshine and scattered showers, luck but shrewdness as well.* There will be someone missing for a while. Give someone the benefit of the doubt.

Tuesday 5th: *People act without thinking. Lots of confidence and style.* If you take part in a committee meeting, don't expect much co-operation.

Wednesday 6th: *There's a new broom. People jockey for power. A good time to settle a deal.* A good friend is going his or her own way, and you won't see so much of each other.

Thursday 7th: *There's a sexy mood, plus some shyness. Which will triumph?* In romance there's some tension, though it can all be eased away by laughter and loving kindness.

Friday 8th: *A moment of success in romance – or freedom from imprisonment.* You mix up with people with emotional problems. You'll feel drained by the end of the day.

Saturday 9th: *Quite happy and creative, with a spot of luck in love or money.* You could enjoy beginner's luck, but know when to call it a day.

Sunday 10th: *Still a close family togetherness. Good links within any group, indeed.* You seem a bit scatter-brained today. It's hard to concentrate on the task in hand.

Monday 11th: *A point of no return. The ending of a chapter, or a fresh start.* There's a meeting with someone important. Make sure you're properly prepared for it.

Tuesday 12th: *Quite a carefree time. People aren't in a fussy* *mood. You'll get on well with everyone.* There's a family duty that mustn't be avoided.

Wednesday 13th: *A day when romance matters a lot. Not a day for taking people for granted.* There's an air of disappointment today, though the evening should make up for it.

Thursday 14th: *Still a restless, travelling mood. There is some deception, too.* Try to keep your good humour. There are great links with the United States in some way.

Friday 15th: *After the gloom of recent days, the desire to have a good time.* There's nowt so queer as folk – as you'll find out today! People aren't as co-operative as you'd like.

Saturday 16th: *Still lucky. There's a glow of well-being round many people.* A name to do with holidays, optimism and luck could prove lucky for you!

Sunday 17th: *If you're the inventive type, you could have a brilliant brainwave!* A relative could be feeling poorly. You want to take a risk, but others urge caution.

Monday 18th: *Still jolly. There should be several moments of luck today.* At work there are delays, and perhaps a shake-up in the work-force. Good time with the family.

Tuesday 19th: *Some sadness around. People can't get through to each other.* You need company. It's a good day for having a few people round for coffee or a drink.

Wednesday 20th: *A stable state of affairs will abruptly alter. Lots of warmth and aggression in romance.* A mechanism could let you down. You won't be able to repair it on your own.

Thursday 21st: *Quite a difficult time. Expect an explosion of rage, or lots of criticism.* Don't leave cash where a light-fingered person could be tempted.

Friday 22nd: *An extravagant time. If in doubt, spend! A great time to make new friends.* A horse whose name is linked with friendship will be lucky for you.

Saturday 23rd: *Some air of deceit today. Information is unreliable. But the family has something to celebrate.* The weekend looks jolly, especially if there have been tempers recently.

Sunday 24th: *Good news for some. Still not a restful time for the world.* You are feeling stand-offish in a romance, and won't want to be taken for granted.

Monday 25th: *More cheerful day or two but arguments still break out.* The weather brings extra worry. There could be a nasty virus waiting to be caught.

Tuesday 26th: *More friendly – also more devious! Outsiders are given a chance.* Be generous to others. Lots of kindness from your nearest and dearest.

Wednesday 27th: *Still cheerful. Good time to force through a deal. But there's one area of doubt.* Your sleep will be disturbed, so you're feeling dog-tired.

Thursday 28th: *Some anger and short temper, but it will soon blow over.* Don't hurry a task calling for creative effort. You should have plenty of perseverance.

Friday 29th: *You could be deceived by someone normally trustworthy.* If you take a small risk, there will be an unsuspected reward. A local entertainment will be marvellous.

Saturday 30th: *Some guilt feelings. A quiet day, good for picking up the pieces.* Tomorrow is best spent quietly on your own. Too many people will bore you.

Wise Words for September

We poison our lives with fear of burglary
and shipwreck – and, ask anyone, the house is never burgled
and the ship never goes down.

Jean Anouilh

October
Guide

Maybe you've been a bit absorbed in yourself in the last couple of months, and now you are more concerned with the wide world beyond.

You could be playing a role in politics, the community, a local protest campaign or whatever. This may coincide with your partner's attitude, or it may be something that you are drawn into by someone else's enthusiasm altogether. If so, this will bring you two closer, and arouse some jealousy elsewhere.

In mood you seem quite lively, inquisitive, keen to explore ideas and very drawn to history, travel and adventure.

WORK. It's a good time to be laying foundations for new growth, especially if you run your own business. You will be keen to map out a new future for your company in 1990, especially if you are venturing into a new field.

In an ordinary nine-till-five job, there may be a worry over working conditions, and these will get worse before they get better. There may also be a new boss or supervisor with whom you don't get on.

It won't be easy for you to win the co-operation of others, especially if a group of work people are rather entrenched in die-hard attitudes.

HOME. No big problems on the domestic front, and if anything the various members of the household will go their separate ways in October, without necessarily seeing a great deal of each other.

Marriage partners in particular are likely to pursue their own interests, with both of you out and about in the evenings and weekends. You won't feel this a threat to your marriage, though your partner may be more worried.

It's a good time to continue decorating, and perhaps be given – or offered at a bargain price – some furniture, carpets or curtains that can be adapted to suit your place.

HEALTH. A busy, bustling vitality takes over your life in

October, and though you may blow a fuse, I doubt if you will rust out!

There could be one digestive problem in mid-month, but you will survive it perfectly comfortably.

MONEY. Pay bills promptly, if possible. There is a chance that one of them – or a bank statement – could contain an error in your favour, so you'll have to decide whether to be honest.

If you're in charge of the family allowances, you may have to be more generous from now on, especially if a teenager is going to college for the first time.

The second half of October is quite lucky for gambling, though the first half could bring a few losses. Avoid investments in oil, gas or chemicals. They are likely to fluctuate wildly in the next six months.

LEISURE. Although you seem very busy in education, politics or some social business, you won't have too much time for pure relaxation.

You may not be able to get round to tidying up the autumn garden, and things that you normally like to do yourself – like car maintenance, for instance – may have to be left to experts. The same applies to dress-making, crafts and hobbies.

You could be making quite a long journey this month – if so, all goes well, and its purpose is achieved.

LOVE. You may witness the break-up of someone else's marriage or long-term love affair, and make you treasure your own all the more. Even so, as I said earlier, you may both be in an independent frame of mind.

For some Taureans an old flame may cross your path and try to cause some mischief. Frankly, I don't think you're interested in going back to an old situation. At present you're much more interested in the future, and if you've had a good relationship going for a number of months, your thoughts may be turning to engagements and marriage.

You get on well with Leo and Sagittarius, but not so well with other Taureans – nor Cancerians, for that matter.

October
Key Dates

Sunday 1st: *Good weekend for travel, so long as you're prepared for surprises.* You mix with another family, and enjoy yourself. Someone is silly in your eyes.

Monday 2nd: *Quite an air of obstinacy. A nice surprising romance, though.* You'll see an old friend again. You have to deal with a stubborn, ignorant type.

Tuesday 3rd: *A cynical, worldly-wise time. Relationships are at the point of no return.* Taurean women are looking for a bit of fun, and will enjoy being chatted up.

Wednesday 4th: *A restful day. Still a danger that you're being deceived.* Snuff out a minor bout of ill-health before it gets a grip on you. Lucky numbers: 5, 8.

Thursday 5th: *Good co-operation, especially at work, sport or enterprising situations.* With money you're a bit of a fool. Look after your health, as it could be getting poor again.

Friday 6th: *Toughness comes back with a bang! Could mark the end of something important.* You have a perfectly good idea, but someone else will find fault with it.

Saturday 7th: *Edgy time for a while, but you'll enjoy getting right away from daily cares.* A good friend is going his or her own way. Someone thinks you're being irresponsible.

Sunday 8th: *A loving weekend. There's a lot of sensitivity in the air.* Plan an exciting entertainment to take place in the next couple of weeks. Enjoy yourself with a friend.

Monday 9th: *An intense day, when one relationship really seems to matter.* Be ready to move fast in a small emergency. Someone acts perversely, cutting off a nose to spite the face.

Tuesday 10th: *A day when many small things go wrong. Not a relaxed time.* There could be a surprise arrival. A decision of yours will meet with general approval.

Wednesday 11th: *One set-back to your plans, but there's luck as well.* Someone will try to stand in your way, but you should be firm and persistent.

Thursday 12th: *Hurry things along. Life is moving too slowly.*

Stubborness in a romance. Ask a small favour by all means – but a big request will have to be turned down.

Friday 13th: *An explosive time in love. Expect a financial surprise, too.* With a bit of luck you'll be paid a super compliment. I wonder why? Lucky colours: gold, red.

Saturday 14th: *Quite a lucky time. Good for romance, partying and friendliness.* All your Taurean tidiness comes to the fore. You'll want to polish and scrub the place clean.

Sunday 15th: *You'll manage to get over a set-back. Finances are a problem.* Something could frighten you today, though it's mostly in your own mind. Lucky numbers: 5, 6.

Monday 16th: *A down-beat day. You won't feel like getting much done.* Your taste is changing. What you loved once will seem boring now. People keep you waiting.

Tuesday 17th: *Could be the end of a chapter in life. You'll bid farewell to someone.* Lucky time is mid-afternoon. Good links with Aquarians and Pisceans.

Wednesday 18th: *You'll try a new way to get what you want. A day of high feelings.* You are confused about what people want from you. It is a day of high passions, with tempers flying.

Thursday 19th: *A slippery time when it's tempting to tell a lie. You may have to wriggle out of a mistake.* Plan a couple of changes at home, and say goodbye to something old.

Friday 20th: *Quite a lucky day. You should feel you're riding the crest of a wave.* An idle remark could send shivers down your spine – but don't let it really worry you.

Saturday 21st: *A happy, creative time, terrific for enjoying yourself.* If you've recently had a shock, take life easy. There are lovely spiritual links in your life.

Sunday 22nd: *Hard-working weekend. Delays likely. Irritation in the family or another group.* Any links with the air are favourable at the moment. There's a bit of rough and tumble.

Monday 23rd: *Basically a lucky time. If in difficulties, there will be a lucky break.* There will be cross words, which can be laughed off. Try to act wisely, not impulsively.

Tuesday 24th: *Deals are struck. A day of good fortune and new possibilities.* Your mood is positive – indeed, you may run into some marvellous luck.

Wednesday 25th: *Quite a mixed-up time. People blow hot and* *cold, not knowing what they really want.* At work, a junior will soon move ahead, which upsets you.

Thursday 26th: *Sexy and enjoyable, but things could turn nasty on the spur of the moment.* The family is in good shape, so you can put a worry to one side.

Friday 27th: *The end of the working week, and not an easy time for many folk. Expect delays and disappointments.* It's a specially good time for Taurean men. Someone makes a fuss of you.

Saturday 28th: *Zippy day, without any great problems. Several nice changes in the offing.* Visitors at the weekend are a mixed blessing! Don't rely on public services.

Sunday 29th: *Could be trouble while travelling. Another day when everyone wants to let rip.* A good weekend for meeting new people, and perhaps patching up an old quarrel.

Monday 30th: *A day of low spirits and anxiety. But travel goes well today.* You are in a warm-hearted mood this evening, full of affection. You'll envy someone else's marriage.

Tuesday 31st: *Pleasant ending to the month. Plenty of vigour and cheerfulness.* You're waiting for news – today, tomorrow and quite a while to come! Lucky numbers: 3, 7.

Wise Words for October

Flirt: a woman who thinks it's every man for herself.
                                                              Anon

November
Guide

You may regret having taken things a bit too quietly the previous month. By being a bit slothful, several opportunities may have slipped by, or else you may realize that things were actually easier in October, and now the tide is flowing somewhat against you.

Ideas formed now may not be acted upon straight away – more probably in early 1990, in fact. Your natural caution stops you from being too impulsive, especially where pulling up roots in concerned.

How you get on with your parents, children, brothers or sisters, where you are living or want to live in the future, and which of your friends become an extension of your family, so to speak – some or all of these questions may be buzzing around your mind this month.

WORK. There could be someone new at work who seems to instill a spirit of enterprise into many of the other staff. There is a very go-ahead, dynamic and prosperous mood at work. The only pity is that you don't seem to share the general enthusiasm.

The financial rewards of your work will be uppermost in your mind. It's a good time to discuss salary changes – but do so in an open, frank manner that won't annoy anyone else.

You may have a special responsibility to fulfil around the second week. But a couple of weeks later, you may find that a decision of your own will rebound on you.

HOME. Deep in your inner heart you will be working out how you want your domestic life to change in the next few months. If you've recently made a move you'll still be busy decorating, buying new furniture (especially for the kitchen) and perhaps making one or two structural alterations.

If your marriage is a struggle of power, then your partner seems dominant at present. So there could be some tension at home.

You'll be quite glad that children are growing up, but sorry that you do not seem to exercise influence over them so strongly as before.

HEALTH. Once again you may see an inherited illness – that is, minor ailments that one of your parents or grandparents often used to catch.

There is also a problem, if you have been over-working, of a sore throat or a boil on the neck.

MONEY. The unexpected can occur. This isn't so much the answer to a punter's prayer as much as a deserved bonus linked to your career or a handsome rebate from the government. Investment opportunities that have been thin on the ground will arrive thick and fast, with a notable upturn in Industrials. If you have a collection of anything, from coins to model soldiers, their value will increase significantly around now.

LEISURE. It's not an easy month in which to plan your leisure hours. Your working time may be somewhat erratic, for one thing, and for another, you may be kept waiting by others, not knowing their social plans.

You may take up an old pursuit you've neglected, and you have fun helping a younger person learn a skill.

If you enter a competition you do well. Visits to friends will also be successful, while a visitor to your house may not be completely pleased.

LOVE. There is definite tension between husband and wife this month, especially if you rarely see eye to eye. At times you may feel the relationship is too much to handle, and you simply want a bit of peace and quiet.

Some Taureans could well be developing a peaceful little friendship which is nice in itself but can never be a replacement for the real thing. The only trouble is that the other person involved could take it a lot more seriously than you do.

Perhaps an office romance could develop this month and become quite serious by the end of the year.

November
Key Dates

Wednesday 1st: *Serious working day. Still a happy time for those in love.* Don't worry about being embarrassed in public; you'll do fine. Lucky colours: white, black.

Thursday 2nd: *Quite a grim scene really. Imagination is getting the better of common sense.* What you enjoy in your spare time won't meet with someone else's approval.

Friday 3rd: *Quarrels are patched up or forgotten. Better for men than for women.* Make amends for any mistake at work. You'll get really enthusiastic and carried away tonight.

Saturday 4th: *Good weekend for travel. A little white lie saves trouble!* You're in a competitive mood, and will want to win. Lucky numbers: 2, 5. Lucky sign: Sagittarius.

Sunday 5th: *Little arguments, but nothing too serious. But people are still inclined to fly off the handle at a moment's notice.* You can still be good company.

Monday 6th: *Good day for tough-minded negotiations. There is a need for some escapist entertainment, too.* If travelling, expenses will be higher than you expect.

Tuesday 7th: *A day of small mercies. Be grateful for them! Slightly sad mood.* Your partner is full of joy, and will try to cheer you up. You cheer up first.

Wednesday 8th: *Still a lively, interesting time, with no big problems. Luck in the afternoon.* A party allows you to meet old friends. Listen to others, but make up your own mind.

Thursday 9th: *Friendly day, with no complications. Still a warm-hearted spirit.* Give the go-ahead to a child who wants to do something different.

Friday 10th: *You'll hear a 'no' when you wanted 'yes'. A day of hard thinking.* A bright idea today will turn into success tomorrow. Good time in your love life.

Saturday 11th: *Not a brilliant weekend. You'll have to settle for second-best.* You can help someone with his problems, even though you're not an expert.

Sunday 12th: *A busy day with conflicting attitudes around you.*

Beware of daft advice. Anyone with the initial S is lucky for you, and may bring good news.

Monday 13th: *Problems suddenly abound. There could be a set-back.* Boredom in your marriage could lead to silent frustration. Warm-hearted evening, with lots of confidence.

Tuesday 14th: *Luckier – and extravagant. Not a day to say 'no' to people.* Your working week will be a strain. A nostalgic time. You may be humouring an old person.

Wednesday 15th: *If people are frustrated, they'll lash out. So don't expect good behaviour.* Get to bed early if you want a really good cuddle! You could win something in a lottery.

Thursday 16th: *Sexy day when you are looking for something different.* Don't give away a secret all at once. A day full of interest. You can help someone with a big decision.

Friday 17th: *The start of a long sexy period! Still a lucky time for many.* Give the go-ahead to a child who wants to do something different. Catch up with paperwork.

Saturday 18th: *Nice family atmosphere – good rapport on the sports field.* A super day so long as you're determined to enjoy yourself. You have to pick the lesser of two evils.

Sunday 19th: *A day to rest and recuperate. Good news about education, travel, holidays.* If you're in a love tangle, things must get worse before they get better.

Monday 20th: *There's lots of co-operation and agreement between folk.* Anyone with the initial F or T is lucky for you, and may bring good news. You get on well with the boss.

Tuesday 21st: *Still a courageous time. Something tricky will go well.* Work now, play later. Get your head down and no day-dreaming on the job. A surprise on the way home.

Wednesday 22nd: *A bad-tempered day, niggly and ungenerous. A time to keep going – without joy.* A child may give you a scary moment, but all ends well.

Thursday 23rd: *More sprightly. A clever, observant day, though with some incompatibility.* An item in the news will arouse your anger. Get on with half-finished jobs.

Friday 24th: *The start of a broadly lucky, successful time in human affairs.* Good time to give up something – you'll find it easier than you fear. Fun with a stranger?

Saturday 25th: *Quite a serious-minded weekend. Good time to* *attend to practical tasks.* There's a money problem to sort out, but don't get depressed by it.

Sunday 26th: *Quite lucky, looking on the bright side. Great for romance.* There may be an argument about something in the past. You can achieve a lot otherwise.

Monday 27th: *Sexy and dreamy at one level. Hard-working and successful at another.* Don't ignore letters, or there'll be bigger trouble in the future.

Tuesday 28th: *Still lucky – also extravagant, easy-going, a great party mood.* Links with church or chapel are warm and friendly. You can establish a new rapport.

Wednesday 29th: *A bit more relaxed, but there are still problems to solve.* A warm and loving evening, when a relationship will become more intimate.

Thursday 30th: *A tough time, but also a serious time – perhaps the right moment for commitment.* In a test of nerves, you won't give up; it's one of your determined days.

Wise Words for November

He hasn't an enemy in the world,
but all his friends hate him.
Eddie Cantor

December
Guide

You seem happy and enterprising at the end of this year. For some Taureans it could be a sharply ambitious time, in contrast to the rather dreary outlook on life in the last couple of months. It's definitely a month to think big, and you'll be surprised at the opportunities that present themselves, even in the Christmas season.

Many Taureans will be dealing with the public in a variety of ways: helping to raise money for a charity, for instance; or taking a keen interest in community affairs once more.

WORK. Problems crop up in the first week, but you have the stamina and patience to deal with them successfully.

In mid-month there's a lovely air of harmony and co-operation, and you get on really well with staff members. There could be one particular person of whom you are really fond.

Just before the Christmas break you must make amends for someone else's mistake, but it's hard to say whether you'll be congratulated – or have to share the blame!

HOME. There could be some arguments among the family in early December, but nearer the holiday a relative has pleasant news to impart, there may even be good news too, about the house itself. Some Taureans will be moving out of rented into private accommodation at this time.

Christmas itself is not quite as vivid as previous years, and you may welcome a chance to get away from family noise for a while. There's plenty of fun with the children, and there could be an especially nice present coming your way.

If you have a second home – a holiday place, perhaps – there could be some alarming news.

You spend plenty of time with another family.

HEALTH. There could be an illness that lingers during the first few days of December, and this puts you behindhand with

Christmas plans. But you'll throw it off in good time for the holiday itself.

If you do suffer from a chronic illness, there may be some lingering aches and pains, but none the less you should feel much brighter and fitter as you bid farewell to 1989.

If you're prone to migraine, the last few days of the year could be troublesome – but remember, exercise mind over matter and the pain can go away!

MONEY. This is always an expensive time of year, but you are more thrifty than usual and don't necessarily feel that you must always keep up with the Joneses.

You seem a little vague about other people's cash. Beware of mislaying money that someone has put in your trust. In particular, you could pocket children's Christmas money.

You could win a friendly bet, but have difficulty in collecting the winnings. You could also sell an old belonging, for a surprising amount of money. You'll feel quite prosperous.

LEISURE. Clearly this is a Christmas when you want to enjoy yourself, but ideally you'll do it rather differently than in previous years. You may take a proper holiday, even abroad, and there won't be quite the emphasis on a family Christmas.

Certainly you seem very sociable, especially from the 20th onwards, and you'll be glad to welcome back old friends into your life. But the emphasis is mainly on making new friends, which suggests that a Christmas away from home is quite likely.

LOVE. Quite a number of Taureans will be plighting your troth around Christmas and the New Year. It's an excellent way of concluding a happy courtship in the last few months.

More probably, however, you are getting yourself into a bit of a romantic fix, especially if there is now an extra-marital entanglement in your life. You are feeling a bit weak-willed about this, with a sweetheart on the side who may be taking the relationship more seriously than you do.

There are happy links with most signs of the zodiac, but especially with Pisces and Cancer.

December
Key Dates

Friday 1st: *The start of a sober weekend. Duty must be followed instead of pleasure.* Don't allow a menace at work to continue much longer. Discuss politics.

Saturday 2nd: *A weekend when feelings get out of hand. There's some deception afoot.* Visitors at home will bring a surprise present. Help a friend with a cash-flow problem.

Sunday 3rd: *Good fun likely. People are in a 'who cares?' mood. Loving and larky.* Someone with the initial H or N could help you. You need a day out in the countryside.

Monday 4th: *An ambitious time. Other people's feelings will tend to be ignored.* A sweetheart wants to ask a favour, but lacks the courage to ask straight out.

Tuesday 5th: *A day of steady endeavour. Not the time to rock the boat.* A talkative day, ideal for exchanging views, making deals, having heart-to-heart chats.

Wednesday 6th: *The start of a marvellous phase for the family. Good luck and travel.* A mechanism could let you down. You won't be able to repair it on your own.

Thursday 7th: *A wonderful mood within the family or in another group.* Put on your best face if going to an important meeting. Some sexual high jinks in the evening.

Friday 8th: *Very lucky in one way, but there's also a drawback.* An impulsive day. Lots of emotional sensitivity, though, so the best of both worlds.

Saturday 9th: *Ideal day to strike a deal, after a lot of argument. A pleasant weekend otherwise.* Too many late nights will hurt your health, so take things easy this weekend.

Sunday 10th: *You may feel a little depressed – but mad as hell, too!* A promise may not be kept, but you don't care. You are quite cheerful, but a child is a problem.

Monday 11th: *A fast-moving day. You'll have plenty of energy and courage.* Two of you can have terrific fun this evening, but three's a crowd. Very powerful sexual feelings.

Tuesday 12th: *Quite a warm-hearted, sexy time. Not a terribly* *loyal day.* Domestic problems will sort themselves out, especially if you're on the point of moving.

Wednesday 13th: *A male relative is a great help. You can get plenty done.* There could be a sad note this afternoon, but you get cheerful again. Hard-working day.

Thursday 14th: *A jolly, laughing day. It's an ideal time to feel free. Perhaps a chance to take time off work.* There's one bossy person in your life. Take things calmly.

Friday 15th: *A more difficult time. Ill-luck will pursue a number of folk.* Romantically your day is hampered by shyness. Go on, pluck up courage – it won't be as bad as you think!

Saturday 16th: *Back to normal. A day when lovers may reach a serious decision.* You'll be busy this evening on boring chores. Shopping will be awful, so avoid it if possible.

Sunday 17th: *You may have to travel in difficult circumstances. An escapist weekend.* A parent will tell you some home truths. There could be cause for jealousy.

Monday 18th: *Very sexy and life-enhancing time. Great for developing a friendship.* The teasing has to stop. If you rag someone too much, there'll be a nasty backlash.

Tuesday 19th: *Slippery and devious day. Someone does the dirty, and there's tension.* Try and get a moment to yourself, to plan where you're going. Very busy time.

Wednesday 20th: *A bit more cheerful and lucky. Not a loyal day, though.* A clandestine romance is favoured, and could go a step further. Lucky numbers: 2, 10.

Thursday 21st: *A warm and friendly day. Good for business, sales and committee work.* There's the chance to use other people's belongings. An older relative needs special help.

Friday 22nd: *A change of pace. New proposals for an appeal. Very modern and go-ahead.* You should be getting on top of a difficult situation. Beware of the shark who smiles!

Saturday 23rd: *Plenty of affection within the family. A group wants to reach agreement.* You'll hear a long story – only half of it is true! A terrific night for a party.

Sunday 24th: *An excitable day full of chatter and good cheer.* Your partner may be moody, so that you must shoulder extra tasks. Otherwise a lovely Christmas Eve.

Monday 25th: *People need to be out and about, visiting and* *keeping everyone happy.* Your advice will not be heeded, but losing your temper afterwards won't help. A bit fraught.

Tuesday 26th: *Vigorous day, with people going off on tangents. Poor concentration.* Mid-week sees a better mood. You'll enjoy a day's racing, but not a visit to other relatives.

Wednesday 27th: *There will be domestic re-arrangements, just after Christmas.* Slimming is an uphill battle today. You'll still be eating and drinking yourself under the table!

Thursday 28th: *People will try to move faster than you want. Perhaps there's teasing in the air.* You may be kept waiting by others. Music and dancing seem called for.

Friday 29th: *Finances are tight at present. People may be soft-soaped to get something from them.* You're asked to do something you find embarrassing. Have fun away from home.

Saturday 30th: *A good day to plan things for next year, but there's an air of exhaustion.* There could be some emotional disillusion in your life. Could be a sad evening.

Sunday 31st: *You could enjoy beginner's luck. A well-to-do person could be generous.* You will have to arrange your plans to suit others. But still a good New Year's Eve.

Wise Words for December

My doctor is wonderful. Once, in 1955,
when I couldn't afford an operation,
he touched up the X-rays.
Joey Bishop

Learning
More

I do hope you have found this book interesting and useful, and maybe your interest in astrology has been truly aroused. Perhaps you can see that in-depth astrology is more fascinating than Lucky Stars columns in newspapers.

All the same, this book applies to everyone who is born under Taurus, whatever the age, sex, social class, job or marital status – and obviously it can't deal with individual problems in an individual way. For that you need something else.

That's where my Starlife astrology service is ideal. If you have any queries about the book itself – and if you want a personal horoscope, based on your own date and place and time of birth – do get in touch with me at the address given at the top of the order form opposite.

The standard report is still the **Birthday Horoscope**, if you want a detailed analysis of current problems and where your life is moving in the next twelve months.

But you might well be fascinated by **Who Were You?**, which looks at reincarnation through the eyes of astrology. Or there's the **Biorhythms Diary**, ideal if you are training for sport, trying to lose weight, interested when (or not when) to try for a baby, or simply wanting to be aware of the daily ebb and flow of energy through you. If you have savings to invest, you will be intrigued by my specialist report **Stars & Shares**.

And of course if you want to see how astrology affects your character, you need your own **Zodiac Portrait**.

Whatever you want, apply direct to me, using the application form on the next two pages. If you live abroad, please pay by bank draft or international money order in £ sterling. Delivery will be about three weeks, and be assured that it will receive my personal attention.

ORDER FORM
Starlife, Cossington, Bridgwater, Somerset UK TA7 8JR

Service	√	Price
Birthday Horoscope Your Personal forecast for the next twelve months, answering your queries and dealing with any problems you have		UK £9.00 Abroad £11.00
Who Were You? A detailed account, based on your horoscope, of the past lives you may have led, showing how – and why – you have today's personality		UK £12.00 Abroad £14.00
Stars & Shares A personal investment guide, based on years of research, showing when, and with which firms, you can be successful on the UK stock market		UK £25.00 Abroad £28.00
Your Biorhythm Diary A detailed daily forecast for the next twelve months, based on biorhythms and astrology, showing how fit, healthy and aware you'll be		UK £12.00 Abroad £14.00
Personal Cassette An hour-long tape dealing with whatever you want – a child's horoscope, your own birth-chart – with complete individual attention		UK £30.00 Abroad £33.00
Introduction to Astrology An audio-visual course for beginners, showing how and why astrology works. Six hour-long cassette tapes, with diagrams and notes		UK £30.00 Abroad £33.00
More on Astrology A book-list of further reading on astrology plus information on astrology groups		free
Zodiac Portrait A fascinating description of your personality as revealed by the pattern of planets at birth. Covers temperament, career, romance, health		UK £12.00 Abroad £14.00

APPLICATION FOR HOROSCOPE

Surname	Mr Mrs Ms Miss

First name

Address

Birth Details Date [ ] **Month** [ ] **Year** [ ]

Birth-place

Birth-time (if known)

Personal Details – absolutely confidential – ask any questions

Work

Home & Family

Health

Money

Romance